Malo's Complete Guide to Canoeing and Canoe-Camping

Malo's Complete Guide to Canoeing and Canoe-Camping

by *John Malo*

Quadrangle Books
CHICAGO

Library of Congress Catalog Card Number: 69-20158

The lyrics of "The Voyageur's Song" on page 18 are
quoted from *Northland Songs Book 1* by permission of
Gordon V. Thompson Ltd., Toronto.

To my wife, Renee, and to my son and daughter,
Kenneth and Marcia, who have respected
the creative atmosphere and
who have understood the self-imposed exile
from family life required to complete this book . . .
To the companionable men and women and
to the youths who have shared with me
in the paddling, camping, singing, and
learning of skills as well as in the
enjoyment of woods and waters
in sunshine and in storm . . .
I affectionately dedicate this book.

Acknowledgments

This book is, as are most books, the product of many minds and hearts.

Sincere thanks to "Uncle" Don Johnson of Farm and Wilderness Camps, Vermont, and to Dr. Dale McDowell, Northern Illinois University, for research help and encouragement in the labor of the "adventure."

I am grateful to all of the state agencies, national organizations, manufacturers, students, and canoeing brethren who have wholeheartedly fulfilled every request made of them in assembling the contents of this book.

To Adele M. Ries, consultant, my thanks for her indefatigable efforts and steadying counsel.

Contents

PART 1

Adventure Beckons

1

The Ageless Lure
of Woods and Waters

The feeling of exhilaration as your canoe slices through the water in response to your paddling strokes, the feeling of placidly floating in some personal Shangri-La, paddle at rest, mind and body in tune with the water and the wind, are treasured experiences the canoe enthusiast wishes every fellow human being could share. Over the noise of a motor-powered craft, how can one listen to the river's song, to the cry of the loon, to the swish of pine trees? How can one observe nature's creatures undisturbed in their native haunts?

The canoe endows its devotees with a unique freedom, a retreat to the simple life, unspoiled and clean, beyond the harsh vibrations of the crowd. Once afloat and in rhythmic movement, the canoeist be-becomes an unfettered spirit, at peace with himself and the world. He can marshal his reservoirs of energy for his return to daily living.

Few modern sports can be identified more closely with the development of the North American continent than canoeing. Few can enhance communion with one's companions and with the wild creatures of quiet places, while offering an opportunity for strenuous and purposeful activity.

The Seminoles in Florida and the Choctaws in the Gulf of Mexico states traveled in dugouts, and the mountain men and the Indians of the West used skin boats (bullboats), with willow frame, all made by their own hands. The trails of the birchbark canoe (from which our modern canoe stems), which carried first Indians, then explorers, missionaries, trappers, and now, recreationists, remain relatively unchanged after three hundred years; and they continue, in sparkling purity, through miles upon miles of undisturbed beauty.

Indians Canoeing shows the small model of the birchbark canoe being paddled by an Indian couple, with their child as a passenger. (PUBLIC ARCHIVES OF CANADA)

The United States and Canada offer a paradise of primeval woods and waters for the canoeist with adventure in his soul. These historic canoe trails weave along silver paths through wild, silent domains, where every turn of the watery highway reveals a new and different landscape—palisades of pine high above rugged shorelines in the north woods, nostalgic pastoral scenes not far from houses in the populated lowlands.

Since the latter part of the nineteenth century, the canoe has served as a recreational watercraft without peer, and today its resurgent popularity lures adherents of all ages to the blue water trails. Perhaps the younger among them will come to enjoy some of the boating experiences of an earlier generation: floating in a canoe while strumming a ukulele in a park-pond serenade; paddling on a willow-fringed lagoon with a sweetheart seated amidships, deep in waterproof cushions, looking only at the paddler; grouping canoes together in the middle of a lake at evening, singing.

The Fox River at Yorkville, Illinois, illustrates the canoeing potential near a megalopolis. Ninety minutes from Chicago's seven-million population complex, the Fox River makes it possible for the canoeist to embark upon a 24-mile stretch of water that offers: varied scenery of field and forest, bluffs and caves; a red cedar tree, recently cut down by vandals, that may have been the oldest living thing east of the Mississippi River; the Indian battlefield at Maramech Hill, where, in 1730, three hundred Fox Indians were annihilated by white settlers; the remnants of an old stone mill; outcroppings of rock from the Cambrian age, five hundred million years ago; a 30-foot waterfall on a feeder stream; the first known permanent Norwegian settlement (Norway, Illinois) in North America; a sulphur spring surrounded by a health spa; five species of evergreen and many varieties of ferns, mosses, liverworts, and wild flowers.

As the canoeist, cruising the silent stream cradled by inclines, half-closes his eyes, he can recall the feats of the intrepid explorer, Robert Cavelier de LaSalle, who, approximately one hundred years before the Declaration of Independence was signed, paddled the same watercourse. As Henri de Tonti wrote in his account of LaSalle's expedition in 1683:

> . . . but a league or two from the river, the most beautiful country in the world, prairies, woods of mulberry trees, vines, and fruits that we were not acquainted with. . . . Their country is very beautiful having abundance of peach, plum, and apple trees, and vines flourish there; buffaloes, deer, stags, turkeys, are very numerous.

Many wild areas on our continent remain to this day and offer the opportunity to observe the "woods and templed hills" as they did to LaSalle so long ago.

Most of the villages, towns, and cities of our country were founded near water. Hence almost all population centers are still blessed with their own adjacent equivalents of the Fox River, where canoeists can find adventure and recapture their zest for living. Local rivers, lakes, lagoons, farm ponds—it matters not which—are adequate waters for canoeing. After having been initiated on the placid water close at hand, the canoeist can respond to the call of the wild and find heightening satisfaction in extended, more ambitious canoe trips.

The traditional canoe-trip regions, usually associated with the north woods areas, are by no means the only locales for enjoying canoeing.

5

Most state conservation departments offer booklets and guides touting their canoeing potential, each depicting its local blessings of preserved natural wealth.

You will discover in Chapter 20, "Mapping the Adventure," that prairie, farming, and mountain states offer canoeing possibilities, as does Canada, in areas contiguous to the United States as well as in the hinterlands.

One peek at such information will stir the canoeist to car-top his craft and be off. Don't wait! Slide your canoe into the water and answer the beckoning call of adventure!

2

Early American Canoeists

This is an age of atomically propelled ships and submarines, of planes that break the sound barrier, of high-speed carriers of every description. But in some areas of the world, as in primitive times, crude dugout canoes still serve essential functions: they carry jungle-dwelling children of the British Honduras to a school in a clearing; they are used to procure food and for fishing; and they transport natives and goods from one village to another. Those dugouts and the birchbark canoes of the North American Indians are the pinnacles of achievement of watertravel craft evolved by native inhabitants to meet their respective needs.

It is easy to imagine how, through eons, the canoe as we know it today, both as an essential carrier and as a recreational craft, evolved from log to raft (logs lashed together), to hollowed log, to skin-hull boat, to birchbark, to our canoes of twentieth-century engineering and space-age materials.

Log. Primitive man, perhaps in the emergency of a flood or upon the sight of debris carried along by the current, straddled a log, floated, and pushed it along with flailing arms and legs. When he conceived the idea of using a long pole to propel his crude craft, he discovered new realms that had been previously denied him, a landlocked creature.

Raft. Eventually, after puzzling over logs which had become accidentally entangled, and perhaps to fulfill a wish for greater control, the early water traveler lashed together two or more logs. Riding above the water on his new raft-like float, he remained relatively dry. Because his pushing-pole was inadequate in deep water, he was limited until he solved that problem: then some enterprising "rider of the water" flattened the end of an oarlike stick to secure better purchase in the water, and thus took another leap forward in efficiency.

Hollow Log. The dugout canoe, varying in size, shape, craftsmanship, and decoration, has been recorded in practically all primitive waterside cultures. It was fashioned from a large tree, usually one with a soft pith, which men felled by burning its base. Then, to char the core wood, they burned the log with controlled fire, gouged out the center with stone adzes, and scraped until they formed a hollow.

This rough-hewn canoe enabled the passengers to sit low in the cockpit, a position which protected them from splashing waves and provided the advantage of some stability.

Eventually, man added refinements to his watercraft, and shaped the front of the dugout better to cut the water, to reduce splash, to lessen resistance, and to enhance speed.

The size of the dugout was dependent on the size of the trees growing in a given region. From the huge cedars of Vancouver Island, for instance, the Indians fashioned dugouts 60 feet long, 8 feet wide, and 5 feet deep—large enough to carry thirty passengers on whale-hunting expeditions in the Pacific.

The thwarts (or spreaders) in the modern canoe originated with primitive dugout construction. Tribesmen, to make their dugout wider than the diameter of the trunk of the tree from which it was made, poured hot water into the gouged-out hull. To this they added heated stones to keep the water hot and the wood soft and pliable. Carefully, they spread the sides of the dugout farther and farther apart until they attained the desired width. To keep the sides of their dugouts in the expanded position, they inserted spreader braces made of hardwood across the open hull.

Skin-Hull Boat. The cumbersome log boat eventually gave way to the lighter and more efficient frame and skin boat—a circular framework of sticks with willow resiliency, covered, stretched tight, and sewn with buffalo or moose hide. The Indian paddled this light hull, resembling a huge basket. However, its circular shape prevented it from traveling on a straight course, so that true maneuverability was lost, and its high sides made the craft vulnerable to winds.

Indian Birchbark Canoe. The canoe of the North American Indians

8

Emergency
Life
Preserver

Poling
a Log

Log
Raft

Hollow
Log

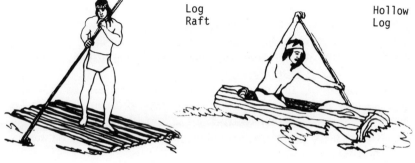

Skin-Hull Boat

Birchbark
Canoe

Primitive tribesmen evolved a craft to solve their problems of water transportation. The versatile birchbark canoe of the North American Indians was adopted by white explorers and fur traders. (DRAWINGS BY ROBERT RUSSELL)

9

represents a long period of development of design and construction. It is the end result of primitive man's years of wrestling with the problem of inland water travel and watercraft.

The nature of the waterways and the use to which the craft was put, plus the availability of materials, largely determined the construction of a canoe. Bark canoes were designed to fit differing conditions— quiet waters, open lakes, rapid river travel, coastal waters. To protect the canoeist from being struck by overhanging branches bordering narrow rivers, a smaller canoe, less high in the sides and flatter at the ends, was needed. To keep from shipping water on long, wide rivers with many rapids and falls, and on open lakes with considerable swells, the canoe had to have high sides and high prows. When the watercourse was menaced by rapids, a light craft that could be carried overland for long distances was the answer.

The various designs ranged from the one-man canoe used for hunting and fish-spearing to canoes large enough to carry a ton of cargo and a crew, a war-party, or families moving to new habitations. Their shape and their surface areas made it possible to turn them, bottom up, for use as shelter at night.

In forest travel, the bark canoe could be propelled easily with a single-bladed paddle. This allowed the paddler to face the direction of his course, to watch out for obstructions in fast-moving, curving streams, and to search for game, quietly stalking it by floating with the current to within bow's range.

The Indians were able to carry heavy cargo in shallow water, and their canoes could be repaired easily in the forest without special tools.

The methods of construction varied greatly between Indian tribes, but the finished craft, with a few regional exceptions, was a functional double-pointed, flat-bottomed, wall-sided canoe, highly developed when white explorers first landed on the Atlantic shore.

The Indian birchbark was made by forming a skeletal frame of flat, thin ribs, closely spaced, and attaching a thin plank sheathing covered with drum-tight bark over these ribs. The gunwales curved outward and upward. The thwarts were always in odd numbers, from three to nine, often with one in the center for balance when the canoe was carried overland.

Ideally, the frame was fashioned of white cedar, because of its characteristic of splitting cleanly and readily when well seasoned. The sheathing over the ribs was made watertight by coating the seams with waterproof gum, the sticky resin obtained from black or white spruce. The long, flexible root of black spruce was the commonly used stitching

10

material, although some tribes preferred to use rawhide thongs.

The North American Indians preferred the bark of the paper birch for their canoes, but when birch was not available, they used other barks—elm, spruce, chestnut, basswood, and cottonwood. The ideal bark came from a naturally straight tree trunk of sufficient diameter and length to give reasonably large pieces. The reported thickness of most barks was that of a French coin, the écu, slightly under one-eighth

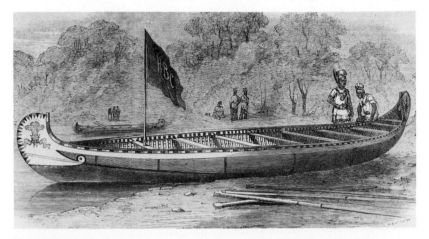

A birchbark canoe is presented to His Royal Highness the Prince of Wales by the Governor of the Hudson's Bay Company, as shown in the *Illustrated London News,* February 9, 1861. (PUBLIC ARCHIVES OF CANADA)

of an inch, a recognizable measure that would communicate the idea to those who had never seen a canoe. During the winter months, the Indians applied hot water to the tree trunk to make the bark pliable. Then, after peeling the bark from the tree, they rolled and stored it for later use.

It is no wonder that the Indian canoe craftsman was highly regarded for his talents. The graceful curve (rocker) of the keel, the upward sweep of the bow and stern, the tight stitching of bark to gunwales, and the ornate work of the finished birchbark canoe presented a craft of utilitarian value and feral beauty.

The white man, arriving in North America, immediately adopted the Indian craft and learned to use it without alteration. In 1603, Samuel de Champlain (who was made Governor of New France in 1627) was the first explorer to record definite dimensions of the Indian bark canoes. They measured up to 23 feet in length, to a 50-inch beam (English measurements), and were capable of carrying a half ton of cargo. He was impressed when his fully-manned longboat was passed by two canoes, each with only two paddlers. Captain George Weymouth of England, in 1603, also noted that canoes, with but two paddlers, could pass his ship's boats manned by his best oarsmen.

The French, at the behest of Champlain, were the first white men widely to adopt the Indian canoe for trade and exploration in the back country. They used Indians as crews because the Indians did not have to be trained. They were able safely to navigate both large and small streams, and to make overland portages quickly. The rapid expansion of the French fur trade, early in the seventeenth century, opened the western country.

Journal accounts in the late 1600's by Père Marquette, Louis Joliet, Chevalier Henri de Tonti, and Baron de LaHotan indicate the massive sizes of canoes—up to 36 feet in length—and the passenger and cargo-carrying capacity—up to two thousand pounds in freight. Their large canoes were fast and safe, and seldom upset.

Fur trading and exploration rapidly expanded, creating a need for many canoes. The Indian canoe-builders were unreliable, and as a result, the first canoe factory operated by the French at Trois Rivières, on the St. Lawrence River, probably came into being as early as 1700.

The most romantic characters in the history of canoeing flourished during the era of fur trading in the United States and in Canada. These were the French voyageurs, who flashed across the northern waters and portaged along forest trails, as the mountain men, the scouts, and the pioneers crossed the plains and mountains in America's westward exploratory marches on horseback or in covered wagons. Every age has its frontiersmen. The young blades living along the banks of the St. Lawrence River in the latter part of the eighteenth century, hearing exciting tales of canoeing in uncharted wilderness to the west, eagerly signed up for the canoe brigades of the fur companies. Although we think of them as colorful and gay, they were durable and industrious, and the typical recruit entered the employ of his masters with a zest for work and a thirst for adventure in unfamiliar land and waters.

The voyageurs, in the main, were dependable young men from stable families. They were short and strong, "born to the canoe," and most were recruited from the parishes around Montreal and the neighboring towns of Laprairie, Pointe Claire, Contrecoeur, St. Michel, Gentilly, and Longueuil. Physical attributes were important, for there was no place in the canoe for the tall, long-legged, heavy employee of the fur trade. Parents along the waterways prayed for children who would grow up to be small of stature, agile, and tough—voyageurs who could carry three times their weight and paddle the whole sunlit day, and often longer. The clothing of the voyageurs was as colorful as their way of life. The canoeist wore a jaunty feather in his red woolen cap, a light shirt, a bright sash around his waist, and deerskin leggings. A bright, beaded tobacco pouch, deerskin moccasins, and hooded coat completed the outfit, for always to be considered were the limitations on weight.

The voyageur's role in probing the unknown fringes of North American civilization by canoe had begun in 1535, when Jacques Cartier (discoverer of the St. Lawrence River) met the Micmac Indians in the area of the Gulf of St. Lawrence, and bartered for the beaver robes the natives were wearing. The popularity of furs in Europe guaranteed a lucrative market: first, for beaver pelts for men's hats; then, for milady's fashions, mink, marten, lynx, ermine, bear, and wolf. Thus was born the fur trade, to flourish in frenzy for two centuries (1600-1800). But the explorations by canoe, resulting eventually in settlements of people, were of far greater value than the initial, strictly commercial enterprise.

Cartier and the voyageurs who followed were responsible for charting the St. Lawrence River and its tributaries— the great and direct watery entrance to the unknown fastness of the northwest. Continued traffic down the water trails eventually opened up new lands, and led to more discoveries of natural treasures, which in turn were responsible for Canada's development and the settlement of the Great Lakes country.

Of Jacques Cartier, poet Thomas D'Arcy McGee wrote:

> . . . And the rills and rivers sing with pride
> the anthem of the free;
> How the magic wand of Summer clad the landscape
> to his eyes,
> Like the dry bones of the just
> when they wake in Paradise.

Horses, oxen, and covered wagons were useless in the north woods: fur trading and explorations were possible only because of the great *canot de maître* (literally "master," or large, canoe) fashioned of birchbark. Probably perfected under the influence of the Algonquin Indian craftsmen, the large canoe had many ideal qualities: its overall length of 36 feet, a beam of 70 inches, and the depth amidships (from the bottom of the canoe to the top of the gunwales) of 32 inches, were typical dimensions. The size of the freighter canoe was complemented by a narrow bottom, flaring sides to prevent splash, sharp ends, a relatively straight keel-line bottom, and a high prow. The yellow bark, free of wrinkles, was made watertight at all seams by amber gum, and the stems were painted with a red and brown representation of the craftsman's totem—heron, wolf, deer, triangle, circle, or other symbol.

A *Canot de Maître* (master, or large, canoe), carrying passengers and cargo on the Northern waters, is manned by the hardy voyageurs. (PUBLIC ARCHIVES OF CANADA)

Such a sleek craft was capable of carrying up to three tons of trade goods, baggage, and provisions, yet that efficient canoe weighed so little that four voyageurs could easily shoulder and carry it to the loading dock.

Diaries of early explorers tell of huge *canots des maîtres* being loaded with this list of cargo, for use both by the enterprise and in bartering for furs with the Indians: awls, axes, gunpowder, gun tools, brass wire, flints, lead, blue Canton beads, blankets, combs, firesteels, guns, garters, spruce gum, birchbark, powder horns, tomahawks, hatchets, hats, kettles, fishline, Hembro rope, hooks, fish nets, mirrors, needles, ribbons, brandy, wine, tobacco, pipes, paint, and false hair.

Boxes fitted with hasps and padlocks, called "cassettes," were used to carry cash and other valuables. Those well-contructed boxes were each the size of an apple crate. They were made of seasoned pine, dovetailed, strapped with iron, and with tightly fitted lids. Also carried were a traveling case, a padded box for medicine, refreshments (liquid) for the officers, and emergency articles needed quickly on the travel route.

14

At ice-breakup time each year, the highly organized fur-trading operation began at Montreal with brigades of large canoes (*canots des maîtres*)

Voyageurs Shooting the Rapids in a freighter birchbark canoe, on Lake Superior en route to Grand Portage. (PUBLIC ARCHIVES OF CANADA)

loaded to the gunwales with bartering merchandise, each propelled by eight to fifteen voyageurs.

The voyageurs, with their red paddles flashing, sent the large canoes hurtling across the water; and when the wind was right, an oilcloth sail helped them along. There was an urgency to the schedules: the men were always fighting against time, for the sun of the seasons was their time clock, and there was no margin for leisure.

No less than fifty miles a day were expected from the paddlers, and any time lost because of accidents, extreme weather conditions, or other reasons, had to be made up. To keep up with the predetermined schedule, the men sometimes drove the canoes for twenty hours without stopping. They pushed on through the dangerous rapids and the windswept reaches of the Ottawa River, Georgian Bay, and Lake Superior, toward the Grand Portage, on the northern shore of Lake

15

Superior, where the cargo they carried had to be delivered for transfer to the smaller wilderness-traveling canoes.

With Montreal seven weeks behind them, the voyageurs' rhythmic paddle strokes brought them to Hat Point. Rounding it, they cruised into the Grand Portage post amid cheering whites and Indians, and to the salvos of cannons. As soon as the large canoes were beached, immediately the reloading chore began. The hundreds of items of merchandise had to be repacked and stowed into the small *canots du nord* (north canoes) which were better adapted to travel the far-flung expanses of small lakes, wild rivers, rapids, and waterfalls that led to the distant destinations of Lake Athabasca, the Mackenzie River—to the shores of the Arctic Sea.

The Grand Portage bay had no outlet to the river system that the voyageurs traveled: the men had to carry all the merchandise and every canoe along a nine-mile portage over a height of land to the Pigeon River—the door to the wilderness. Two ninety-pound packs, along with personal duffle, composed the minimum load for each crew member. To help them carry such heavy loads, the voyageurs used a tump-line—a flexible strap from the bottom of the pack to the forehead. With his body bent forward to counteract the weight, the voyageur would have an extra bag of duffle, or a keg of spirits, added to the top of the load, where its own weight kept it in place. Thus heavily loaded, the voyageur would set out on the long carry at a brisk pace, and not once stop: then he would return to the beginning of the portage for another load. The average burden was 250 pounds, and no self-respecting voyageur would carry less. For extra pay, some would carry three packs. The great Negro voyageur, Bonga, could handle five; and seven pieces, 630 pounds, have been known to be "toted" over the nine-mile path of mud, clay, rock, and sand. At the end of the portage, the men loaded and balanced the light canoes by carefully stowing the cargo: cassettes, baskets of bread, bags of biscuits, kegs of spirits (rum and high wine), tins of beef, pemmican, tents, personal duffle, and bedrolls. They covered the cargo with a heavy, oiled tarpaulin, and with shouts from the "guide" in charge of the brigade, the canoes would be off.

In 1768, Grand Portage became the crossroads of the fur industry on the continent, and for over a hundred years furs were exchanged there. Normally there were a thousand Indians camping outside the palisades of the fort; but on occasion, when a general assembly of the tribes was held, as many as ten thousand would come by trail and by birchbark canoes from the Lake-of-the-Woods country and from distant

Unloading a North Canoe (freighter) at a trading post. Note the details of the voyageurs' practical dress and the flexible tumpline (strap) from the bottom of the pack to the forehead. (MINNESOTA HISTORICAL SOCIETY)

Saskatchewan. Then they held pow-wows and traded their pelts. White, as well as Indian, traders came from as far west as the Great Plains, the Oregon country, and down from the bleak tundra beneath the Arctic Circle. The high excitement of the short rendezvous there, during which voyageurs drank and sang with old friends, white and Indian, and told tales of distant places, would end abruptly. The small canoes had to be inspected, maps studied, crews assigned, and destinations determined. The local priest blessed the men and the canoes, "au revoirs" were

17

shouted, and once again the voyageurs entered upon their assigned tasks.

During those summer months, the voyageurs would push their canoes, carrying them over land areas, paddling the waterways, penetrating farther and farther into the hinterland, suffering from bad weather, sickness, bugs, and possible crack-ups while shooting the white water. As the land rose and fell, the smooth water roared into ruffled disorganization, and decisions to shoot the rapids or "to take out" had to be made quickly.

Those men had a great respect for their birchbark craft, the lifeline of their fur and exploration enterprise. More often than not, when white water was sighted, the commander ordered a "traverse" or portage. As the canoe touched the shore, the first man out quickly made a fire, set a pot of water on it, and proceeded with the back-packing of duffle. Just before the men made their final trip portaging their gear, the fire-maker added tea leaves to the now boiling water, and the voyageurs drank the stimulating beverage. After that hasty pick-me-up, they would be off, with little time wasted. The kegs of spirits posed problems on portage trails, and being practical men, the voyageurs made certain of consuming their ration before coming upon too many carries—usually accomplished early in the trip.

Hardships in many forms came to the "green" voyageur on his first trip: few hours of sleep, hastily prepared meals, back-straining loads, physical exhaustion, and exposure to the elements. Upon becoming a seasoned "man of the woods," conditioned to the environment, he would sing and whistle with the veterans.

The songs of Old France, like the chanties of the seamen, rang across the waters to the stroke of their paddles. The men sang away the pangs of hunger, the back-breaking weariness, the cold sting of the spray on their faces.

> Ho! for the life of a voyageur!
> Ho! for the haunts of game and fur!
> We drive along the old canoe
> And comb the bank for beaver.
> Ho! for the tumbling rapids' roar!
> Ho! for the rest on lone lake shore!
> We live beneath the old canoe,
> And sleep beside the river.

Singing as a morale-builder was acknowledged by the officials of the fur-trade enterprise, who rewarded a man with a good voice with extra pay.

As the days passed into weeks, and with Lake Superior behind them,

18

the canoes fanned out in all directions: to Ile à la Crosse, Cumberland House, the Red and Mackenzie river areas, and Lake Athabasca. Those were the fur-trade routes, but some canoe brigades pointed their prows in directions other than beaver haunts: to the prairies by way of the Winnipeg River, the Upper Mississippi, Green Bay, the Fox and Wisconsin rivers, Lake Michigan, the Illinois River, and the Lower Mississippi.

Although the birchbark canoe had made possible the marriage of the Atlantic Ocean with the Great Lakes, the Arctic Ocean, and the Mississippi River, and contributed directly to the growth of two great nations, not one remains today to be enshrined in a museum. The simple birchbark craft was constructed not of timber, hide, or metal. Its delicate components, after making their heroic contribution to the culture of Canada and the United States, moldered away.

The actual routes of the voyageurs still remain, many of them unchanged by the population explosion, by industrialization, technology, political upheavals, and wars. The portage trails that knew the moccasined tread of Indians and voyageurs, the panoramic vistas, the bodies of water, currents, winds, insects, and birds, have scarcely changed since the time of the fur traders—and for that matter, not for seven thousand years.

In this twentieth century, we can identify with the pioneers of the waterways as we master the skills of paddling modern canoes, as light as their birchbarks. Enjoying a hearty outdoor meal, relaxing around a campfire at the end of a day's cruise, we share the satisfaction of the voyageurs in the knowledge that we, too, have brought safely through a day of travel the crew, the canoe, and our duffle.

3

~~~~~~~~

Words and Terms Canoeists Use (A Glossary)

Canoeing, like other sports, hobbies, and activities, has its own vocabulary.

Many of its words and phrases have been adopted from the language used for other watercraft down through the centuries. Most beginners are familiar with a number of basic expressions, such as "fore," "aft," "bow," "stern," "beam," "gunwale," etc.

To enjoy conversation about this sport, and to be able to communicate immediately with fellow paddlers without hesitation or repetition, most canoeists use commonly accepted technical words. There are some regional variations, such as coastal or midland-lake enunciations and phrases, which canoeists would do well to learn and use.

This basic list of words should be of help in familiarizing you with the words used to describe the craft, its accessories, and canoeing activities.

Abeam........................at right angles to the center line (that runs from prow to stern) of the canoe.

Accessories.................additional equipment, usually demountable and replaceable, that adds convenience, comfort, safety, or completeness.

Aft..............................toward the back or stern of the canoe.

WORDS AND TERMS CANOEISTS USE (A GLOSSARY)

Ahead..................ahead of the canoe.

Alongside dock..........a pier, high bank, or rocky ledge offering enough depth of water to bring the canoe parallel to the shore for loading and embarking.

Amidships..................the middle section of the canoe.

Astern..................behind the canoe.

Bailer..................a scoop for dipping water from the canoe.

Bang strip ....also called "stem band": a protective half-round metal strip on the outside of either end of the canoe, extending from the point of the deck to the keel.

Beam..................the width of the canoe at its widest part.

Blade..................broad, flat surface of a canoe paddle.

Bow..................the front portion of the canoe.

Bowman..................the person, paddler, or passenger who occupies the front, or bow, seat.

Broadside..................the side of the canoe extending its entire linear dimension from the bow to the stern.

Bush..................wild, uncleared, roadless country. "To go bush" is to revert to a wild state.

Carry..................see "Portaging" below.

Catch..................see "Purchase" below.

Deck..................the flat triangular pieces of mahogany, aluminum, or ash on top of the bow and stern ends of the canoe, to which the gunwales converge and attach.

Depth..................height of the canoe from the bottom to the top edge of the gunwales.

Draft..................same as "Draw" below.

Draw..................the depth of water that the canoe displaces when floating. When the term is used in connection with stroking a paddle, it refers to the blade's being parallel to the center line of the canoe, as it is pulled in (in-draw), or pushed away (out-draw).

Duffle..................the essential apparel and equipment for a particular situation carried by the canoeist. Also called "Gear."

Forward..................toward the bow or front of the canoe.

Freeboard..................the distance from the water line to the gunwale.

Gear..................see "Duffle" above.

Grip............................the top end of the canoe paddle. Now comes in varied shapes: the Indians used no special grip. See also "Purchase" below.

Gunwales...................pronounced "gunnels." Two hardwood strips (mahogany, spruce, oak, or ash) that bracket the ribs and extend along both upper edges of the length of the canoe. The inner strip is called the "inwale," the outer one is the "outwale."

Hinterland.................undeveloped back country far from urban areas.

Inwale.........................see "Gunwales" above.

Johnboat....................a long, flat-bottomed, and square-ended craft used mainly on shallow rivers.

Keel............................a narrow hardwood strip that runs along the bottom is called a "lake keel"; its design, projecting down into the water, prevents sideslipping in the wind or current. The "shoe" or "river keel" is a wide flat strip, giving a larger margin of safety to the canoe's bottom, and allowing it to sideslip in fast water.

Lake Keel..................see "Keel" above.

Leeward.....................the direction toward which the wind is blowing; opposed to "windward," which is the direction from which the wind is blowing.

Lift.............................see "Rocker."

Line............................the rope, also called "Painter," used to tie up, tow, or track a canoe.

Lining.........................pulling a canoe around rapids, etc.

Outwale......................see "Gunwale" above.

Paddle........................a relatively short oar with a wide blade at one or both ends, used to propel a canoe.

Painter........................see "Line" above.

Planking.....................on wood-canvas canoes, and on all-wood canoes, the thin boards, generally red cedar, covering the outside of the ribs over which filler is applied.

Pontoons....................detachable floating members, as hollow cylinders, balsa wood, or buoyant plastic, rigged to crossarms outboard of both gunwales.

Portaging...................the carrying of canoe and duffle overland between navigable waters.

Port side....................the left side of the canoe facing forward.

22

WORDS AND TERMS CANOEISTS USE (A GLOSSARY)

Prow..................the front end or cutting edge of the canoe.

Purchase..................the fast hold of the paddle blade in the water preparatory to stroking. Sometimes called "Catch," or "Grip."

Ribs..................strong curved strips of wood, nearly always made of white cedar wood, that run in single length from gunwale to gunwale—bent down at the sides and across the bottom.

River keel..................see "Keel" above.

Rocker..................the slight rise or rocker curves at the bottom of the bow and stern sections of a canoe that serve to lift the canoe over the waves and white water, and prevent plowing into the water.

Rope..................also called "Line" or "Painter": see "Line" above.

Shaft..................the round, narrow portion of a canoe paddle between the grip and the blade.

Sheer..................the upward sweep of the bow and stern from amidships of the canoe as seen from a side view.

Ship water..................water inside the canoe from leaks or splash.

Solo..................a lone paddler.

Sponsons..................air chambers built into the gunwales and running the length of the canoe.

Spreader..................see "Thwart" below.

Starboard side..................the right side of the canoe, facing forward.

Stem..................the curved piece of wood protected by a metal strip at the bow and stern ends to which the planking, gunwales, and decks are attached.

Stem band..................see "Bang strip" above.

Sternman..................the person who paddles or operates an outboard motor from the rear or stern portion of the canoe.

Thwart..................a brace or crossbar of strong wood (oak, mahogany, ash, or spruce: also called a "spreader") that extends across the top opening of the canoe from gunwale to gunwale. Usually three in number.

Tracking..................a substitute for portaging a canoe around rapids or falls. Lines are attached to the bow and stern ends of the canoe, which is then pulled and guided around obstructions.

Trim............................the angle at which the canoe rides. Especially important when canoe is fully loaded and the bow rides slightly higher than the stern.

Tripper.......................a traveler who canoes for recreation.

Tumpline....................a strap, with padding at its pressure points, that is secured around the chest or forehead to help support a pack carried on a person's back.

Water line..................the line to which the surface of the water comes on the side of the canoe, indicating the degree of submergence when the craft is fully or partially loaded.

Whitecap....................the wind and wave condition that causes a white foam crest to form on fast-moving waves.

Windward..................the direction from which the wind is blowing: as opposed to leeward, the direction toward which the wind is blowing.

Yaw...........................to sway or deviate unintentionally from the intended course.

Yoke..........................a paddled frame fitting that is anchored to the gunwales at the point of balance so that a canoe may be shouldered while it is being carried upside down. Many modern canoes have permanently fixed yokes attached to the canoe.

4

~~~~~~~~~~

Rent, Borrow, or
Buy Your Canoe

From the canoe of the American Indian, with its frame of cedar ribs covered with paper-thin tree bark, to modern aluminum and plastic models, the canoe has remained unaltered in basic design and efficiency.

The birchbark canoe of the Indian floated upon the water "Like a yellow leaf in autumn, Like a yellow water-lilly," according to Longfellow's *Hiawatha*. Its light construction in graceful lines, a primitive work of art, enabled the Indian quietly to stalk animals, birds, and his enemies along the rivers and bays, to explore areas where food might be more abundant, to seek out suitable seasonable environments, and easily to transport his family and his goods when necessary.

Having inherited the Indian design, modern man has used his ingenuity to develop a canoe that has all the advantages of the birchbark creation and additional safety features.

The shape of the canoe provides its versatility: pointed at either end, the canoe quietly and efficiently cuts the water, pushes it aside, and then permits it to return to the stern with little disturbance or wake. The craft draws little water, requiring only a shallow depth for flotation, and its shape enables the paddler to move forward with a minimum of effort. Whether the canoe be paddled, poled, sailed, or powered with a small outboard motor, the shape of its hull enhances movement with ease and smoothness. If the hull is well designed, then the greater the

25

ratio of length to width, the faster the craft will be. The longer canoe is faster than the shorter one of the same basic design: it has more stability, can hold more, draws less water, holds its course more steadily, and paddles faster.

A canoe of the correct size for its intended use, properly loaded and balanced, its operators equipped with the simple skills of handling and always using common sense, justifies the tag, "safest craft afloat."

There are two basic shapes of modern canoes: the original double-ender (pointed at either end) and the one with a square stern for the

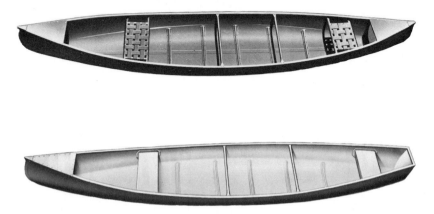

The 15-foot aluminum double-ender weighs approximately 75 pounds, and the 17-foot approximately 80 pounds; the 16-foot square-ender of the Rich Lines weighs approximately 80 pounds. (RICHLAND MFG. CO.)

attachment of a small outboard motor. The most popular lengths in use today generally run from about 13 feet to 20 feet.

The factory-made canoe has installed seats, but some experts prefer the paddling thwart—not for sitting, but for bracing the back while paddling in a kneeling position. Veterans who use the canoe extensively prefer to paddle from various kneeling positions. They claim that kneeling gives them more freedom since their position in the canoe is not dictated, and by being low in the canoe they get better leverage on the paddle. To the recreation-minded canoeist who is only an occasional tripper, however, the seatless canoe is uncomfortable—in kneeling, the flexed position of the knees puts stress on unused thigh and trunk muscles, which complicates and detracts from the pleasure of the weekend enthusiast.

A few decades ago, only all-wood and canvas-covered canoes were available. Today, the use of uniquely adapted modern materials makes available many types of construction, resulting in sleek crafts of beauty—light and durable.

The first step for the canoeist planning to rent, borrow, or buy a canoe is to choose the design and size suitable for the use he intends to make of it.

Canoes are constructed of different materials, and each has its fervent supporters. One should consider an objective, overall view of the most popular types.

PARTS OF A CANOE

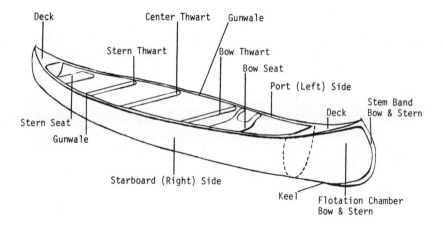

The aluminum canoe has all the advantages of the birchbark canoe— flat bottom, pointed ends, large load capacity, and stability—yet it is lighter than wood, plastic, composition, or canvas. (DRAWING BY ROBERT RUSSELL)

THE ALUMINUM CANOE

The aluminum alloy canoe has developed mainly into a pleasure craft that has the advantages of the birchbark—lightness, sturdiness, and durability.

The construction process starts with a rectangular sheet of aluminum alloy, much longer than the proposed finished length. The sheet is

27

clamped between hydraulic jaws, then stretched and fed into a die on a stretch press for coldforming of half of a canoe. The bowed half-canoe form is then placed in a holding fixture, where it is drilled, deburred, and trimmed to shape. After this it is tempered in an oven at high heat, to give it adequate toughness and rigidity.

Parting the waters with an aluminum canoe. Even the dog enjoys the sport! (GRUMMAN ALLIED INDUSTRIES)

The two halves are riveted together. The installation of the pre-formed reinforcing parts—thwarts, seats, and decks—is included in the 2,000-rivet operation. To assure watertightness of all seams, a neoprene tape and waterproof compound are used between all riveted hull parts.

After careful assembly, the canoe is lowered into a large tank of water to make sure that there are no leaks in the riveted-hull seams. The finished natural aluminum product is a sleek craft with graceful lines and proportions.

Providing flotation for the metal craft is the next operation. Styrofoam blocks are built into the bow and stern chambers to increase the canoe's buoyancy and to make it virtually unsinkable. Should the canoe become filled with water, it will tend to stay upright (as do most canoes) and remain floating indefinitely, enabling the passengers to ride it ashore, or to clamber aboard, bail out the water, and resume paddling.

To eliminate the bare look of the pressed and riveted metal, and to cut down the reflected glare of the sun, the aluminum canoe can be painted. This is best done when the canoe is new. A coat of corrosion-inhibiting zinc chromate primer should be applied at the factory if the canoe is intended for salt-water use.

The finished 13-foot canoe with a 35-inch beam weighs approximately 45 pounds, and supports a load of 760 pounds. At the other end of the scale, a 20-foot double-ender weighs 115 pounds, and can support a maximum load of 1,600 pounds.

All models, when fully loaded, draw little water, a feature which enhances their maneuverability.

It is obvious that the modern aluminum canoe incorporates all the advantages of its birchbark ancestor: pointed or narrow ends, a flat bottom, large load capacity, and stability. The metal canoe can be shaped into proportion, line, and design difficult to achieve in the frame type of canoe with its sharp bending-of-ribs construction. The aluminum canoe, being lighter than wood, plastic, composition, or canvas, is ideal for portaging and car-top transportation. It glides smoothly over rocks and snags, and resists punctures, rips, and tears better than any other type of canoe. The minimum maintenance necessary for an aluminum craft is its selling point. This canoe can be left outdoors in all seasons, year after year, without damage. It is not affected by extreme temperatures; it is impervious to rot; and it will not warp or dry out. It is understandable, therefore, that approximately two-thirds of the canoes manufactured in the United States are made of aluminum.

Consider some of the disadvantages of the modern metal entry into the canoe field. The forming of the shell of an aluminum canoe requires extremely expensive dies, jigs, and fixtures, which prohibits the production of numerous models. Therefore, the range of design types is somewhat limited.

Canoe purists, like the veteran skiers who object to metal skis, criticize the aluminum canoe for the tinny slap-slap sound of waves against its sides, its appearance of cold, hard, stamped, and riveted metal that glints the sun, and its limited range of models. Its critics also claim that the aluminum canoe absorbs heat from the sun and becomes hot to the touch (if left unpainted); and, in cold weather, the metal's coldness can be transferred to the feet and to the knees.

Brushing aside the disadvantages as minor, thousands of happy, satisfied owners of aluminum canoes claim that this canoe's many excellent features and the lifetime guarantee to the purchaser, more than compensate for its shortcomings. Also, they add in rebuttal, that Canadian Indians and white trappers, whose livelihood depends on the canoe, are now buying aluminum canoes. Canoe-rental outfitters, resorts, and camps stock few other types of craft. For them, the aluminum canoe is representative of our era—as sleek and modern as this year's automobile.

THE CANVAS-COVERED CANOE

The canvas-covered canoe probably came into being when an explorer, in the latter part of the nineteenth century, punctured his birchbark craft, and rather than scrounging for birchbark, patched it with canvas or cloth available in his packsack. The patch, it was discovered, held up as well as or better than the original birchbark. The logical follow-up was to cover the entire canoe with canvas, rather than be encumbered with a doubtful supply of material that split easily, dried out to brittleness, and had little permanency.

The unique shape of the canoe frame—pointed at the end, the upward sweep of the bottom and gunwales, the flared sides—required a versatile material to cover these curved skeletal areas. Canvas proved to be an improvement over birchbark: it could be smoothly stretched, its strength enabled the craftsman to apply great force to a small area, and a concentrated pull over sharp curves made for a skintight covering.

The construction of the modern canvas-covered canoe directly parallels that of the Indian birchbark. The frame construction is basically the same (discussed earlier) as the bark creations—white cedar strips, red cedar planking, spruce, oak, or ash gunwales, mahogany or oak decks, oak or ash stem, and oak, ash, or spruce thwarts. A form is built, then the inwales, inside stem, ribs, and bottom planking are laid and fastened with rust-proof nails. The skeleton frame is then removed from the form, and the decks are wedged fore and aft, attached to the inwales and stem (the curved bow and stern member). Next, the side planking is nailed to the ribs, and bent to the stems, nailed, and trimmed. The thwarts, or cross braces, are then put into place to firm up the open skeleton into a rigid form.

The wood-framed seats are caned, and are bolted low enough in the canoe to assure stability. The seats are removable, because in rough

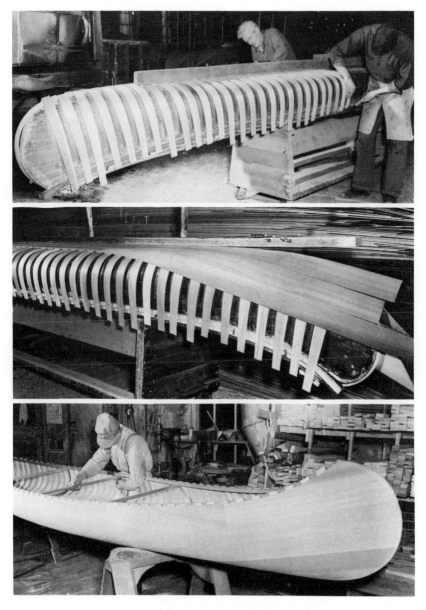

Top: Expert craftsmen shape the ribs around a canoe form, the first step in building a canvas-covered canoe. *Center*: Planking is being tightly fitted over the ribs and clinch-nailed to them. *Bottom*: Thwarts are secured before the canoe is covered with canvas and fitted. (OLD TOWN CANOE CO.)

31

water, the removal of seats allows the canoeists to kneel or sit on the bottom, which provides greater stability.

The canvas used for the canoe covering ranges from No. 4 (very heavy) to No. 15 (very fine and light) cloths. The No. 8 seamless canvas is the most popular and the most commonly used. The canvas is made smooth and waterproof with fillers, such as white lead, and with other recently developed plastic products that give a flint-like surface. The high-gloss paint job is then covered with waterproof varnish, and no traces of the canvas texture remain visible. The canvas-covered canoe has the advantage of a variety of colors, beautifully rendered and highly resistant to fading. All exposed wood, sanded to show the natural grain, is varnished in a high gloss and hard finish.

On the outside, from end to end along the median line of the bottom of the canoe, a strip of wood called the keel is attached with brass screws. Three types of keel construction are offered. They range from no keel at all to one keel an inch high, with in between, a flat shoe keel a half-inch high. The type of keel is determined by the intended use of the canoe. Freighter canoes have additional bilge keels on each side of the center keel, for added strength and protection of the canoe bottom.

The component wood parts of the canvas canoe are naturally buoyant, so that it requires no built-in flotation. It will not sink when upset unless it is heavily laden with some fast-sinking cargo that is trapped by the seats or the thwarts.

The canvas-covered canoe has its disadvantages too. It requires regular care in the form of proper storage, repainting, revarnishing, and recanvasing. On long trips, the canvas can absorb water; also, a new paint job adds weight. The canvas tears on rocks and snags, and on extended cruises it is necessary to carry a patch kit.

The canvas-covered canoe is the most popular type in Canada, and it has many fervent adherents in the United States and in Europe. Because it is the direct descendant of the Indian creation, it is the choice of many veteran canoeists. There is also the appeal of its being fashioned by skilled craftsmen to resemble most closely the original birchbark. Reasons given for selecting this type of canoe include: the greater selection of sizes, because they are hand-crafted, not molded; the flexibility of the bottom and the silent cruising factor; and the pleasing touch, sight, and smell of wood, canvas, and varnish.

The manufacturers point out that the extra fullness at the bow and stern enables the canvas-covered canoe to ride large waves instead of cutting through them as does the canoe with sharp ends. The canvas-covered canoes' versatility makes them ideal for cruising, sailing, and carrying heavy loads. They are dependable on large rivers, lakes, ponds, and salt water.

THE FIBERGLAS CANOE

Fiberglas, light, flexible, and durable, has been discovered by the canoe manufacturers, and they are using the material in imaginative

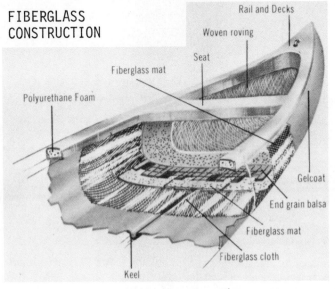

FIBERGLASS CONSTRUCTION

Rail and Decks

Woven roving

Seat

Fiberglass mat

Polyurethane Foam

Gelcoat

End grain balsa

Fiberglass mat

Fiberglass cloth

Keel

(OLD TOWN CANOE CO.)

canoe construction. The fiberglas engineers envision the canoe of the future (fiberglas, of course)—without ribs, planking, or external covering—featuring a long, sleek, one-piece hull that will be the lightest of all canoes and practically indestructible.

Presently, fiberglas canoe construction consists of molding two layers of woven-glass cloth and one layer of "glass mat," bonded with a resin adhesive to which color has been added to give permanent color. The addition of color pigment to the mix allows a wide range of color possibilities. Different colors on the gunwales and on the hull make possible two-tone combinations.

The molded construction, similar to that in aluminum canoe fabri-

33

cation, eliminates the need for a skeleton of ribs and planks, making possible a smooth, flat floor. This, along with the elimination of thwarts (cross bracing), gives more open space for increased cargo and passengers.

A 16-foot fiberglas canoe, an unsinkable craft, floating upright with one deck out of water and the hull flooded. (OLD TOWN CANOE CO.)

The springy fiberglas construction, molded with pliant, adhesive resins, permits flexing of the bottom, in tight quarters, to approximate closely the handling advantages and supple qualities found in the original birchbark and in canvas-covered canoes.

Strength in the fiberglas canoe and stability afloat are guaranteed by the extra lamination on the bottom. Adequate flotation measures are added, with foam-type plastic inserted in the bow and stern chambers of the canoe. The woven-glass construction of the hull gives a toughness impossible to puncture.

The processes of fiberglas construction vary widely among different manufacturers, but all agree that their product is "as tough as steel," and that fiberglas is the canoe material of the future.

Die costs, forming presses, and the exorbitant outlay of capital required for a mass-production operation, which results in a high price for each canoe, are the present drawbacks to the popularity of the fiberglas canoe. In time, it is claimed, these disadvantages will be eliminated, and, eventually, the new canoe will compete with the aluminum and canvas-covered types.

THE ALL-WOOD CANOE

A canoe which is hand-crafted by artisans and is becoming an heirloom akin to a vintage automobile, is the all-wood canoe. It is a rare creation of rib and ship-lap construction, made so watertight that no outside covering is necessary.

A molded mahogany canoe with diamond-shaped waterline and two outer veneers of mahogany surrounding two inner layers of tough Swedish birch, once crafted by a builder of Olympic racing hulls in Sweden, is no longer being made. It is now rarely seen, and, to this writer's knowledge, there are only three available at one dealer in the States.

The Canadian Strip Cedar Canoe, with tapered keel and brass bang plates, finished with natural varnish inside and out, is produced in very limited numbers in Canada. It is available through at least one distributor in the United States. Standard equipment for both their 16-foot pleasure model and their finer-line regatta competition model of the same length includes floor boards, rawhide laced seats, center thwart, brass bang plates, tapered keel, and two paddles.

SUMMARY OF NEW CANOES

In the canoe-manufacturing industry, the counterparts of the automotive giants—General Motors, Ford, and Chrysler—are the highly regarded Chestnut Canoe Co., Ltd. (of Canada), the Old Town Company of Maine, and Grumman Boats of New York. These, and other fine upcoming companies, some of whose names and addresses are included at the end of Chapter 5, spend great sums of money on research to bring about a better craft. The design considerations, engineering, construction, and material testing assure complete satisfaction to the modern, discriminating customer.

Canoes made by reputable manufacturers are, in the main, excellent products. Every model on the market indicates a demand for and a satisfaction on the part of fans, based on the needs which each craft fulfills: recreational—quiet paddling on a pond or lagoon, canoe-camping, camp waterfront, fishing, hunting, racing, running white water; and commercial—hauling freight, prospecting, trapping.

There is little unanimity of opinion on the relative merits of the various canoes. Read the next chapter on "Design and Specifications," study all available literature to learn about different models, and compare them critically.

THE SECOND-HAND CANOE

Should one, of necessity, consider the purchase of a used canoe, some guidelines help not only to get a sound craft, but also to get the craft suited for the use one plans to make of it.

Why not rent a craft until you have a solid background of experience in maneuvering the type of canoe you would like to own?

1) Keep away from the round-bottomed canoes (unless you are a racing expert) and those with narrow beams or shallow depths.

2) Check the ribs and planking for: breaks that spring outward and bulge the canvas; for rot, particularly on the bottom; for repairs already made and those now needed.

3) Look for deterioration of canvas, especially along the gunwales and keel and under both decks.

4) Should the covering of a canoe be defective, but the hull be sound, it may pay to have it recovered with canvas or fiberglas cloth.

5) Check the paint for blisters and the canvas for cracks, especially at the curves of the bang strip, keel, and gunwales. If you've ever re-canvased a canoe, you realize the pressure placed on the canvas at these contours.

6) Compare the canoe's present weight with the original specification* to get an indication of the coats of paint which have been applied to date.

7) Check molded canoes for breaks and hairline cracks. Make certain that the hull is not sprung out of its original shape.

8) Consider buying only a canoe made by a reputable manufacturer. Shun all homemade creations.

---

*Obtain a catalog from the company which manufactured the craft, and read the original specifications.

LEARN TO PADDLE IN A RENTED CANOE

While learning stroking skills and gaining increased confidence in your ability to control your craft in a rented canoe, you can be investigating the different kinds and makes of canoes on the market. It is not necessary to purchase a canoe. Canoe rental agencies are mushrooming all over the country, especially near water that lends itself to the enjoyment of canoeing—a lake, a reservoir, a lagoon, or a portion of a river—where a canoe is rented, used locally, and returned to the dock of the livery. In general, the charge for canoe rental varies from $3.00 to $5.00 a day, with cheaper rates on weekdays. In Scotch Plains, New Jersey, Ted Miller, owner of Bowcraft Sport Shop, along with renting canoes, maintains a two-acre shallow pond behind his store, where beginner canoeists can practice their stroking in safety.

All canoe liveries are not located close to the water. Some of the most popular are far from the water's edge. Rental services include car-top carriers, tie cords, and paddles, for any period of time from one day to several weeks. Many of their customers are vacationing families bound for some favorite lake or stream. Most operators located on a river offer a pick-up service to take canoe and passengers upstream to a launching site. This eliminates the need of backtracking a route, and also enables the canoe party to travel farther in a given period of time. The fee charged for picking up a canoe party varies with the length of the trip. The operators use cars with car-top carriers for single-canoe pick-ups, and small trailers with canoe racks for large parties, such as church groups and Scout troops, using several canoes. A pick-up from a 10-mile canoe run is approximately $2.00; a 30-mile run usually costs $4.00 for the party.

The modern canoe rental livery maintains a fleet ranging in size from a half-dozen to several hundred canoes. Ray Snider of Grayling, Michigan, makes his livery, on the famed Au Sable River, a full-time business renting his fleet of 135 canoes. Bruce Smith, a Grayling, Michigan, schoolteacher, is in the canoe rental business part-time, with 81 canoes.

Another rental business is the canoe outfitter—located generally on the highly popular canoeing waters, where vacationers of all ages combine canoe-camping in a wilderness-style experience. From the outfitter, it is possible to rent everything for the canoe trip: canoe, paddles, tent, mosquito netting, packsacks, sleeping bags, air mattresses, axe, shovel, reflector oven, food, maps, etc. In the popular Superior-Quetico canoe country (Minnesota and Canada), the cost for a complete trip is usually $8.00 per day, per person.

Bill Rom, an outfitter in Ely, Minnesota, has increased his rental fleet since 1946 from six to over four hundred canoes. He, like most outfitters, is a local citizen and an expert canoeist. Their free advice and counsel are as important as the equipment for which they charge.

The modern canoe rental enterprise has grown into an imaginative business in the past few years. A most versatile canoe rental enterprise is the Chicagoland Canoe Base, with sales and rental of over fifty models ranging from an 8-foot canoe for solo paddling, to a 34-foot voyageur canoe for eighteen passengers. The fiberglas copies of the original birchbark north canoe of the fur trade are in great demand for pageants and historical reenactments of early explorations.

The National Canoe Rental Directory, listing over one hundred liveries from coast to coast, is available without charge through Grumman canoe dealers, or through writing to Grumman Boats, Marathon, New York 13803.

5

Canoe Design and Specifications

Before making his selection and buying a canoe, a canoeist should become acquainted with the range of sizes offered by manufacturers. The prospective buyer should also consider some of the basic principles of good canoe design. He should be aware of the fact that, in some cases, emphasis upon the advantages of one feature may mean the sacrifice of some other element.

TYPICAL SPECIFICATIONS OF THE MOST POPULAR CANOES

Length	Beam	Depth	Weight
13 feet	26″ to 36″	11¾″ to 12¾″	45 to 55 lbs.
14 feet	32″ to 34″	11¼″ to 13″	55 to 60 lbs.
15 feet	30″ to 37″	12″ to 15″	45 to 70 lbs.
16 feet	30″ to 36″	12″ to 16″	50 to 80 lbs.
17 feet	35″ to 45″	12″ to 17″	55 to 115 lbs.
18 feet	33″ to 46″	12″ to 18″	60 to 130 lbs.

As he explores the market for the purpose of buying a canoe, the canoeist need not be confused by the total range of sizes. These run from 11 feet to 13 feet, smaller than the most popular sizes listed

A 15-foot pleasure canoe with a canvas-covered cedar hull. (CHESTNUT CANOE CO.)

above, and, beyond them, the 18- to 26-foot lengths. Obviously, manufacturers have reasons for providing each specific size.

Canoes up through 15 feet in length are used largely for solo paddling, especially by children, because of their advantages of being light and easy to launch and paddle.

The 16-, 17-, and 18-foot canoes are ideal, and most popular, for both solo and tandem paddling. They are preferred by the American Youth Hostelers, by personnel of wilderness camps, by outfitters, fishermen, and canoe-campers (who must carry heavy loads and possibly a third passenger). These lengths respond well to a small outboard motor.

Two models new in 1968. *Top*: A 15-foot molded fiberglas canoe. *Bottom*: A 16-foot molded fiberglas canoe. (CHESTNUT CANOE CO.)

This range of canoe sizes has an adequate beam of at least 36 inches to go with the 13- to 18-inch depth which assures a safe freeboard and stability. They are easily carried over the portage trails.

EXCEPTIONAL SIZES

The large Indian war-type canoes ranging up to 30 feet and propelled by eight paddlers are used today in special recreational situations and in historical pageants, as well as in summer camps. The modern war-canoe type is built with heavy planking and ribbing covered with canvas or fiberglas colored to simulate the original birchbark.

A 22-foot freight canoe with canvas-covered cedar-hull construction. This craft is popular in the Canadian North, where it is used for freighting supplies. Its broad beam of 60 inches gives it a tremendous carrying capacity. (CHESTNUT CANOE CO.)

Many of the other canoes longer than the 18-foot class are used for purposes other than recreation. There are many men, in sections of the northern United States and in Canada, whose lives revolve around canoe transportation—for freighting foods, goods, and building materials to wild roadless regions; for commercial fishing, hunting some animals for food, and trapping others for their fur; and for prospecting for valuable ores. The canoe used in these pursuits must be large and of suitable strength, of great depth, and of wide beam, with thick planking and heavy ribs spaced close together. The requirements and standards of this working craft differ widely from those of canoes intended for week-end and summer sport.

41

SOME BASIC PRINCIPLES AND DETAILS OF GOOD CANOE DESIGN

In general, a well-designed canoe has a long hull, for the greater the ratio of length to width, the more efficient the performance and the greater ease in paddling. Long hulls of good basic design, in contrast to short ones, provide more stability, have greater capacity, and draw

BOW END DETAILS OF A CANOE

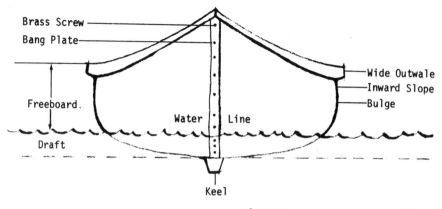

(DRAWING BY ROBERT RUSSELL)

less water. The long canoe's semi-elliptical, wide, and shallow surface (the underside in contact with the water) gives a large wetted surface that enables it better to hold a course. It can be paddled faster than the shorter models. The ideal hull has sharp entry lines that split the water, pushing it to either side in graceful waves, and then permitting it to return, at the stern end, in an efficient water-displacement action.

The bottom of the bow and stern ends rise slightly from the keel, to give lift to the canoe, enabling it to cruise above the waves without plowing and without splashing water over the bow deck and the sides.

Steering is also improved by the rocker-like curve of the canoe's bottom. The canoe that is curved ("rockered") in slight degree, paddles more easily than one with a perfectly straight bottom.

In canoe design, stability is achieved at the expense of speed. The

42

wide, flat-bottomed craft is stable. The narrow canoe with a rounded bottom is designed for speed.

A long canoe with narrow knifelike ends will respond faster to the paddle, but it will lose maneuverability by cutting into waves instead of rising above them.

Nature has a way of being difficult when it hurts the cruising canoeist the most. Many times when the schedule requires steady forward progress, the wind and the waves and the current buffet the

MIDSHIPS CROSS-SECTION OF A CANOE

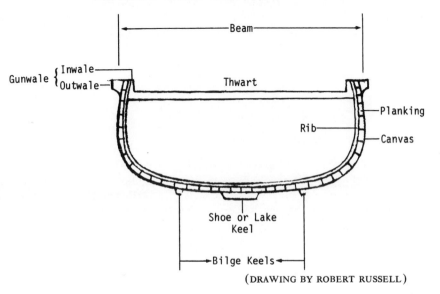

(DRAWING BY ROBERT RUSSELL)

long canoe, causing it to ship water, soaking the cargo, and endangering stability. The paddlers must stop making progress to bail out the water at their feet. Canoes with high prows and sides will be affected by wind, but in high waves they will be less likely to ship water. Canoes without seats (or with seats temporarily removed) compel the paddler to kneel, which lowers the center of gravity for safety and provides better leverage for more power in stroking.

The secret of efficient propulsion is for the canoeist to have a craft the right size for the load usually carried. For example, a 17-foot canoe will paddle more easily than a smaller one with the same combined weight of duffle and occupants, because the smaller canoe will sit lower in the water, and that will impede its progress.

BUYING YOUR CANOE

The canoe-buying situation is unique. Many companies make canoes, but few are put on display for the general public. Local boat dealers usually stock only a single make. Hence it is difficult to get an overview of the many styles, lengths, and types on the market. Visit all boat dealers in your area to check on the variety of models available. If the displays and the information are inadequate, write to manufacturers for their literature. All firms will sell direct if no local representative is situated in your area.

Canoes made by well known, reputable firms have all reached a high level of quality. The competition among manufacturers has kept the selling price pretty much in line.

Table of Approximate Canoe Costs

Since labor and material considerations cause constant changes in the cost of manufactured goods, it is difficult to indicate the specific price of a canoe. An approximation can be ascertained from the following prices—from major canoe companies—of a standard 18-foot canoe.

STANDARD TYPES OF CANOES

18-foot	Double-end canoe	Wood-canvas	$310
18-foot	Double-end canoe	Fiberglas	305
18-foot	Double-end canoe	Aluminum	265

In computing the price of other sizes of the double-end canoe, add approximately $15.00 for each additional foot of length, and deduct approximately $15.00 for each foot less than the size indicated above.

OTHER TYPES

18-foot	Sponson canoe	Wood-canvas	$475
18-foot	Square-ender	Wood-canvas	415
17-foot	Square-ender	Aluminum	270

Sponsons can be attached to an assortment of sizes in the wood-canvas models at an expense of $150.00 over the basic price. Square-end canoes are limited to the 16-foot and larger sizes.

SPECIALIZED TYPES

25-foot	War canoe	Wood-canvas	$ 565
26-foot	North canoe	Fiberglas	895
34-foot	Montreal canoe	Fiberglas	1,495
17-foot	Molded canoe	Mahogany	325
16-foot	Double-ender	Ship cedar	325

The specialized canoes are manufactured only in the sizes indicated.

There are freight charges from manufacturer to buyer, and prices are subject to change without notice.

CANOE KITS

The prospective do-it-yourself enthusiast should consider carefully whether or not he or she is capable of achieving adequate standards of beauty, style, and safety in a homemade canoe, designs for which are offered in some magazines. The basic principles of design required great skill for the original creators and their successors to achieve finished crafts. Ask if your finished product would be adequate in balance, seaworthiness, and dependability, or become a dangerous cloth-covered frame?

Some companies offer kits with complete materials and step-by-step instructions and claim many satisfied customers. Among them are Trailcraft, Inc., Glasco, Kansas 67445, who have a Trailblazer line of wood-canvas models: 12-foot, 14-foot, and 16-foot double-enders, and a 15-foot square stern. Their Trailpacer factory-molded fiberglas, offered in either kit form or factory-assembled, includes 16- and 18-foot double-enders and a 17-foot square-stern model. In their Trail-finder line they offer a 16-foot canoe, of factory-molded fiberglas, either factory-assembled or in kit form. They also have 16-foot double-end and a 17-foot square-stern molded-fiberglas, factory-assembled-only models.

Canoe-Manufacturing Companies

Although some manufacturers specialize in the use of a particular kind of construction and construction materials, some are adding others

45

Trailcraft's finished models made from canoe kits. *Top*: Trailblazer wood-canvas models. *Bottom*: Trailpacer factory-molded fiberglas in kit form or factory assembled—16-foot double end, 17-foot square end, and 18-foot double end.

to their lines. For example, Chestnut Canoe Company entered the fiberglas field in 1968.

Here are some companies who will be glad to furnish the names of their dealers in your territory or send you literature, so that you can inspect different crafts and critically compare them. You will find a canoe that should fit your particular needs, and, thanks to the advantages of mass production, one whose price will be reasonable for a lifetime of canoeing pleasure.

Aluma Craft Boat Division
   1515 Central Ave., N.E., Dept. TR, Minneapolis, Minn. 55413
Amenian Fabricators, Inc.
   Kingsdown Road, Box 635, Orangeburg, S.C. 29204
Chestnut Canoe Co., Ltd.
   Fredericton, N.B., Canada
Chicagoland Canoe Base
   4019 N. Narragansett Ave., Chicago, Ill. 60634
Grumman Boat Co.
   Marathon, N.Y. 13803
Hunter Everett Boat Co.
   McHenry, Ill. 60050
Industrial Fiberglas Products Co.
   Ludington, Mich. 49431
Mirro Aluminum Co.
   1512 Washington St., Manitowoc, Wisc. 54221
Mohawk Boat Co., Inc.
   Gardner Lane, P.O. Box 150, Amsterdam, N.Y. 12010
Niagra Polymer Products, Inc.
   232 Woodward Ave., Buffalo, N.Y. 14217
Old Town Canoe Co.
   Old Town, Maine 04468
Richland Manufacturing Co.
   Richland, Mo. 65556
Sawyer Canoe Co.
   4496 North U.S. 23, Oscoda, Mich. 48750
Shell Lake Boat Co.
   Shell Lake, Wisc. 54871
Skaneateles Boats
   Skaneateles, N.Y. 13152
Thompson Bros. Boat Co.
   Peshtigo, Wisc. 54157

Trailcraft, Inc.
Glasco, Kans. 67445
Wagemaker Co.
Market and Rowe Sts., Grand Rapids, Mich. 49505

In 1969 there are over sixty canoe manufacturers in the United States. The omission of firm names from this list in no way implies disapproval, but only indicates the difficulty of covering the range of acceptable canoe manufacturers in the United States and Canada.

STORAGE

Store your canoe in your garage, barn, or basement. Save floor space—hoist it to the rafters with a pulley arrangement, or keep the canoe out of the way on a pair of two-by-four crossbars nailed to a side wall. If you have no choice but to store your canoe outdoors, construct simple racks (in a shady place) to keep it off the ground. Anchor two upright fenceposts in the ground, half the distance of the length of the canoe apart. Attach to each upright a cross member that is a little longer than the width of the canoe, so that the finished T-shaped members face each other. Rest the inverted canoe on the racks, lash it to them, fasten with chains and padlocks.

The same effect can be achieved by the use of two carpenter's sawhorses, placed apart one-half the length of the canoe. The inverted craft should be placed on them and tied down.

Should the canoe be placed directly on the ground, bottom side up, the parts touching the ground—two ends and one gunwale—should be protected by boards or flat stones.

48

6

Paddles and Paddle Care

A canoeist averages 25 paddle strokes per minute, 1,500 within an hour. The paddle as a piece of equipment, therefore, is very important. It should be selected with care, as an extra ounce of weight makes a big difference during a full paddling day.

Good paddles are difficult to find at boat liveries, which stock primarily the emergency type for motorboats. A good outfitter, or the canoe manufacturer, is the best source of well-proportioned, light yet strong, paddles made especially for the canoeist.

Beginners often make the mistake of selecting a paddle with a large blade, feeling that it should take them farther within a given period of paddling—very much like the laborer who asks, "Which shall I use, a large or a small shovel?" That the coal hiker shovels more coal in a work day with the smaller shovel is a proved fact. A canoe paddle blade of reasonable width (six inches) enables the paddler to make good time, and it is less tiring to use. Further evidence is offered by the American Indian; he uses the narrowest of all blades.

A paddle with an uncomfortable grip can cause cramping, slipping, or blistering. If you find the grip of your paddle irritating, use a sharp knife to carve out a modification on it that fits your palm, thumb, and fingers better. It is important to do a thorough sandpapering job on the altered shape.

Accepted guidelines for individual paddle lengths are: for the bow-man, the paddle (from the tip of the blade to the top of the grip) should reach from the toes to the chin; for the sternman, the paddle should reach from the toes to the forehead. The paddle used by the sternman is always longer, for several reasons. The tapering stern end of the canoe gives more stroking water area to facilitate steering. The full view of the canoe from the stern seat offers a constant bearing on the trim and the direction of the craft. His position nearer the tip of the canoe (the bow seat is set back to accommodate the feet) gives max-imum advantage in stroking for sustained control of the canoe's move-ments. The stern paddle can be a bit wider than the accepted six-inch dimension because of the steering responsibility. These combined ad-vantages of position and extra paddle length are logical reasons for the sternman's being the captain of the canoe.

Among strong, experienced canoe men, individual preferences for paddle lengths prevail. Some bowmen prefer a paddle as long as the user's height. Some sternmen prefer a paddle four inches longer than their height, with a paddle blade width of up to seven inches. These standards are recommended only for the experienced canoeist.

Just as there are differences of opinion and personal preferences for types of canoes, so are there many personal opinions about the quality, strength, and weight of the different kinds of wood from which paddles are made. Paddles are made from the hardwood trees—ash, maple, and cherry—and from the softwoods—spruce, cedar, and pine. Con-sensus of opinion, backed by purchases, indicates that the spruce, maple, and ash products are the preferred blades.

As experience increases, most canoeists will decide upon a favorite paddle or "blade," as it is often called. The choice should not be dis-puted. Favorite paddles, like old fishing hats or treasured casting rods, have a way of becoming something akin to a family member. They become a cherished possession, with painted insignia, unique shape, polished finish, that bespeak a pride and respect for services rendered.

The spruce paddle is best for open lake work, where there is plenty of water. Its wood is light and strong, but it will split more easily than will ash and maple—especially when used in sudden violent action such as emergency situations of fast water, high winds, impending collisions, etc. Also, the tip of a spruce blade has a tendency to fray on hard surfaces, such as sand, stumps, and rocks. To restore a fuzzy tip, use a sheath knife to trim it off to bevel the tip, then oil and varnish.

A practically unbreakable spruce paddle is produced by a composite of three pieces of wood welded together. The shaft, extending the full

DETAILS OF A PADDLE

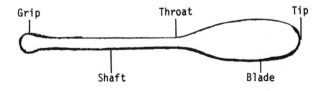

Grip   Throat   Tip

Shaft   Blade

GRIPS:

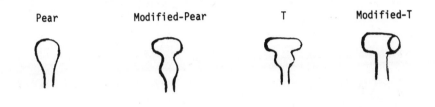

Pear   Modified-Pear   T   Modified-T

BLADE SHAPES:

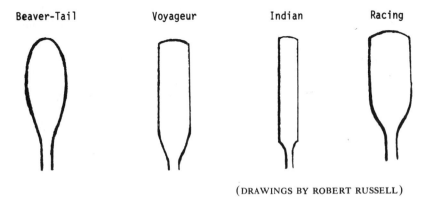

Beaver-Tail   Voyageur   Indian   Racing

(DRAWINGS BY ROBERT RUSSELL)

51

length of the paddle from the grip to the tip of the blade, has a straight-edge grain (like a baseball bat) facing in the direction of the blade's flat surface, where the greatest pressure is applied. The lateral wings of the blade (of flat-grain wood) are glued to the shaft with a waterproof resin glue. The finished blade is not rounded at the tip, but has a straight-sided, square-tipped, racing shape that gives a better purchase in shallow water and more power in deep water. This is preferred by expert sternmen.

The maple paddle is springy, tough, and heavy. To offset the weight disadvantage, it is trimmed down to give a limberness that slices the water effectively and supplies extra whip at the end of a stroke. The maple paddle stands up under the abuse of rocky river paddling and of swift currents, and it is useful as a pushing pole in shallow water. Its shaved-down shape makes it vulnerable to fracture in sudden violent action.

The ash paddle is slightly lighter than its maple counterpart. If constructed of good, close-grained wood, the ash is practically as tough and dependable as maple, and it is less prone to warping.

POINTS TO REMEMBER WHEN SELECTING A PADDLE

1) Check the entire paddle for knots in the wood. A knot indicates a weakness, and the shaft will break under stress.

2) One-piece, mass-produced paddles should be examined carefully for a straight grain running in straight lines throughout its length (like a baseball bat).

3) The composite-type paddle made of several pieces of wood represents a hand-crafted paddle that will stand up better than the mass-produced ones.

4) Because hardwood paddles are heavy, they may have been partially reduced by thinning down the blade and shaft to cut down weight.

5) The beaver-tail is the blade shape most widely used by stateside canoeists. The preferred grip is the pear-shape, although the T-shape grip is claimed by many to be more comfortable in the hand. The early Indian paddles illustrate that the paddle, like the original birchbark canoe design, has changed very little.

6) The experienced canoeist always makes sure that there is an extra paddle each time he boards his craft, in case of possible loss or damage; therefore, consider a duplicate paddle.

EARLY INDIAN PADDLES

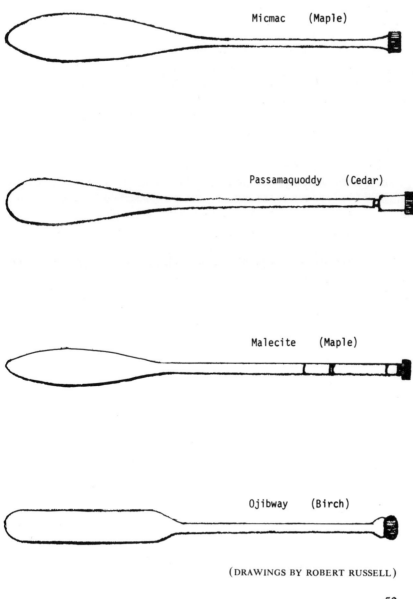

Micmac   (Maple)

Passamaquoddy   (Cedar)

Malecite   (Maple)

Ojibway   (Birch)

(DRAWINGS BY ROBERT RUSSELL)

53

PADDLE CARE

Too often paddles are abused: they are used as slicing boards (while camping), as crowbars, hammers, and shovels; they are thrown on the ground, left exposed to the hot sun, and strewn about the campsite. The paddle should be accorded the same respect and care as that bestowed upon a compass, a first-aid kit, or an axe.

New, unpainted paddles should be rubbed with linseed oil—coat after coat, allowing the paddle to dry thoroughly between applications, until the wood can no longer absorb more oil. After the oiling procedure, apply a coat of spar varnish, allowing it to dry completely. Sandpaper the entire paddle surface with a fine-grain paper, and once again varnish.

Some canoeists prefer to leave the grip untreated.

To prevent warping, wet paddles should not be exposed for a prolonged period of time to the hot sun. If a paddle should become warped, use an Indian practice for restoration: bury the paddle deep in mud, and leave it there for several days. Eventually the paddle will straighten out and return to its original shape.

For winter storage, wipe the paddle clean and hang it up. Avoid storing it flat or tossing it into a corner.

PART 2

Stroke by Stroke

7

Basic Cruising Strokes

The canoe, like any other watercraft, can be propelled forward, stopped, reversed, and made to travel in a circle. The canoe also can be made to move sideways, to spin halfway around so that the bow points in the original direction of the stern. Most surprising, it can be spun completely around on the spot, so that the bow of the canoe returns to its original position.

Novice paddlers need not be disheartened by those canoeists who have become fascinated by involved form, who execute fancy strokes, and who use appropriately impressive language to describe their activities.

Showmanship belongs to the sports amphitheater, filled with spectators who must be entertained and who show their appreciation and pleasure with applause. "Show" strokes, with fancy follow-through, are never seen on remote water areas.

Above the 52nd parallel in Canada, the author watched Cree Indians, unaware of his observation, paddle across gale-torn lakes with short, choppy, but well-timed rhythmic strokes. Under exactly opposite weather conditions, with not one breath of air stirring, with water as calm as glass, those same Crees stalked game in silent movement. In neither case were the strokes concerned with style or beauty: they were practical measures to achieve utilitarian goals.

A survey recently conducted among canoeists listed twelve paddling strokes under sixty-five different names. Of the twelve, only the forward cruising, the turning, and the stopping strokes are essential for the average canoeist. Many of the others belong solely to the realm of competitive racing, to professional canoeists, trappers, hunters, travelers in the hinterlands, and to camp waterfront instructors who, while teaching a group of beginners, must maneuver adroitly between many awkwardly-paddled canoes.

Good paddling can be defined simply as natural movements that propel the canoe in the desired direction, under control. As no two paddlers are physically alike, whether one uses long strokes or short ones is dependent upon the length of the arms, one's basic strength, and the present water-wind conditions. The most natural and comfortable stroke should serve as the main guideline.

There is agreement on the basic paddle strokes which will give control of the canoe in all situations, even though the strokes are called by different names:

Bow Stroke (also known, appropriately, as the "Basic Power Stroke" and the "Straight Cruising Stroke")

J Stroke (also known as the "Fishhook" or the "Steering Stroke")

Guide or Canadian Stroke

Sweep Strokes: "Bowman's Sweep" and "Reverse Sweep"

Draw Strokes: "In Draw" (also known as the "Pull-over") and its opposite, the "Out Draw" (also known as the "Push-over")

Jam Stroke (also known as the "Braking Stroke")

Backwater Stroke (also known as the "J Stroke in Reverse")

Bow-Rudder and Stern-Rudder Strokes

Sculling Stroke

Poling (see Chapter 11, "Outboarding, Sailing, Rowing, and Poling")

BOW STROKE

The bow stroke is the "bread and butter" stroke that moves the canoe forward. This stroke provides the basic propelling action of paddling. In a straight cruising situation, with clear water ahead, the bowman paddles ahead, setting the pace, with absolutely no thought of, or responsibility for, keeping the craft on course by steering. When a canoe's course is menaced by rock, sand bars, or logs, other strokes, explained later, are needed.

When the beginner, therefore, uses the bow stroke, there should be an experienced canoeist in the craft, acting as sternman, making

BOW STROKE

(DRAWING BY ROBERT RUSSELL)

course adjustments with specific stern strokes. With a "crew" in the stern, the beginner canoeist can concentrate on becoming acquainted with the bow stroke and can practice it without worrying about the canoe's tipping, turning, grounding, or breaking up on a submerged rock. He has the added advantage of being able to learn to use the bow stroke on one side of the canoe at a time. In principle, this is little different from the requirements that the Federal Aviation Agency has, that a pilot must have a given number of hours of instruction with a licensed flight instructor before he may fly solo.

Mastery of the bow stroke enhances basic proficiency in other paddling strokes, for most of them are built around the straight bow stroke.

After settling down in the bow seat, grip the paddle shaft with your right hand just above the blade (or slightly higher). Cradle the grip of the shaft in the palm of your left hand to get a loose ball-and-socket mechanical advantage. Check the paddle for the best "feel" of lower-hand position—at the throat or slightly above. This is especially necessary when the proper paddle length is unavailable. It is from this position that you begin the stroke.

Paddling action is simple. It is broken down here for your preparation:

1) Turning slightly to the right, with your right arm thrust forward the blade, which is at right angles to the canoe, keeping the shaft on a vertical plane, being sure not to overreach.

2) Use the upper-arm hand, from the shoulder-chin area, to push the paddle ahead for blade entry into, and suitable "catch" against, the water.

3) You obtain the stroke action from a continuing push forward of your upper (left) arm while your lower (right) arm holds temporarily in an extended position, acting as a pivot to the lever action.

4) You make the paddle blade continue back on an almost vertical plane to drive the canoe ahead.

5) When the paddle blade reaches a point opposite your hip, use your right hand to lift it out.

6) Drop your left hand back toward your waist, causing the blade, which has begun to float to the top, to leave the water.

7) The stroke finished, relax both arms.

8) Return the blade for another stroke by "feathering": turn the blade in a wide arc so it is parallel to the surface of the water, in order to avoid the possibility of digging into the waves and to avoid encountering wind resistance.

Some Fine Points to Remember

1) Keep the paddle close to the canoe, being careful not to scrape your hand or the paddle shaft along the side of the canoe.

2) Do not pull the paddle blade back through the water with the right arm. Push it with the upper (left) arm. "Paddle floater" is what tenderfoot paddlers in canoe-camp classes dub those who pull the blade, not too vigorously, and allow it to float with little power throughout the stroke.

3) Never dig the lower (right) hand into the water. Keep it above the surface.

4) Move the paddle blade through the water in a nearly vertical plane. On this vertical plane, the tip of the blade makes an elongated quarter-circle arc in the water from the moment it dips below the surface until it reaches the point opposite the hip and is withdrawn.

5) The mechanics of the bow stroke can be likened to rowing a boat. The bottom hand acts as the oarlock, while the upper arm pushes against it to move the blade in the vertical quarter-circle arc in the water.

6) Only the minimum rotation of trunk and shoulders, to abet the

J STROKE

(DRAWING BY ROBERT RUSSELL)

most efficient arm motion, contributes to smoothness, efficiency, and endurance. "Body English," lunging into the stroke and using excessive body motion, is unnecessary for the execution of a good bow stroke.

7) There is no advantage to a fancy follow-through: power is neither added nor enhanced by a long stroke beyond the hip.

All the components of the bow stroke will become second nature with practice. As in all habit formation, the actions, at the outset, will tend to be jerky, slow, and fatiguing. With practice and experience, the dipping, stroking, and feathering of the paddle will become a rhythmic action of beauty and efficiency.

J STROKE

The bow stroke, applied at the side of a canoe, causes it to turn from a straight course in the direction of the side on which the stroke is applied. This is one reason why we recommend that the beginner learn to paddle with an experienced canoeist acting as his sternman. As the novice paddles, using the bow stroke, the sternman, paddling on the opposite side, brings the canoe back into a straight line with the J stroke, which compensates for this slight turning action. Even when

61

there are two experienced paddlers in the canoe, the stern paddler will use the J stroke.

The steering, or steadying, quality of the J stroke comes from the finish of the stroke. To execute the J stroke, the sternman twists the paddle when it is opposite his hip, so that the inner blade edge is backward and the blade is parallel to the side of the canoe. A final push outward from the canoe gives a rudder action that offsets the tendency of the canoe to move in a wide arc.

The degree to which the blade should be turned at the end of the stroke, to keep a canoe on course, is determined by the strength of the bow paddler as well as by wind and current conditions.

In strong crosswinds, a J-stroke effect is present when the sternman paddles on the leeward side, and in effect, the power of wind or current helps the sternman's chore of keeping the canoe on a straight course.

Obviously, when any canoeist graduates to solo paddling, he almost continuously uses the J stroke on one side of the canoe, while kneeling in the center of the canoe. Or, after making preparation by adding weight to the bow section for proper trim purposes, he can sit at the stern.

Some beginning soloists meet the problems of the turning canoe by paddling with the bow stroke, first on one side, then on the other, from the amidships position. In that case, he must prepare for this paddling on the left side by making the proper hand adjustments from his right-side paddling. Other beginners use the paddle as a rudder, trailing it at the end of the stroke. Both practices are clumsy and in-efficient, and they interfere greatly with the smooth progress of the canoe, as the J motion or configuration has a braking effect.

The J stroke, properly performed, is a smooth and continuous action, executed with the same rhythm and timing as the bow stroke.

GUIDE OR CANADIAN STROKE

An effect similar to that of the J stroke can be achieved by passing the paddle blade through the water at a slight angle, like that of a boat propeller. The finish of the stroke, a quick, outward flip of the paddle, using the gunwale as a fulcrum, gives considerable resistance to the upward recovery of the blade, and keeps the canoe on a straight course. As the blade makes its sweep on its slight angle, there is some loss in the forward thrust, as there is in the J stroke.

Once this stroke has been mastered, the canoeist will be able to cope

CANADIAN STROKE

(DRAWING BY ROBERT RUSSELL)

with any situation of wind or water. The guide stroke is used almost universally by Canadian Indians and expert canoeists, as it can be used for hours without causing fatigue.

All the foregoing strokes represent the straight cruising strokes, those which move the canoe forward on course.

Mastery of the cruising strokes comes from: (1) using your shoulders and body without swaying; (2) bringing the paddle through in a path that is parallel to the keel of the canoe, without scraping the gunwale or hands; (3) the teamwork of two paddlers, the bowman setting the paddling pace, the sternman paddling and steering to keep on a straight course.

8

~~~~~~~~~

Advanced Stroking Skills

To change the course of your canoe—to turn it in a different direction, to stop its forward motion and propel it backward, to pivot, and to move sideways—use a specific type of stroke to accomplish your purpose. On the whole, these advanced strokes are easier to learn than are the basic cruising strokes (discussed in the previous chapter) which you should have mastered before trying to meet situations requiring the advanced ones.

Knowledge of all the strokes and an awareness of when to use a specific stroke to advantage enhances the canoeing adventure.

These advanced strokes are presented in sets which tell you how to achieve exactly opposite movements of the canoe.

SWEEP STROKES CHANGE THE COURSE OF DIRECTION

Use sweep strokes to change the direction of your course. They provide the leverage that turns the canoe away from its immediate course.

Sweep strokes may be made with either a forward paddling motion or its opposite, a backward (reverse) sweep motion, depending on which way you wish to turn, port side (left) or starboard (right). The type of sweep stroke you execute depends also on which side of the

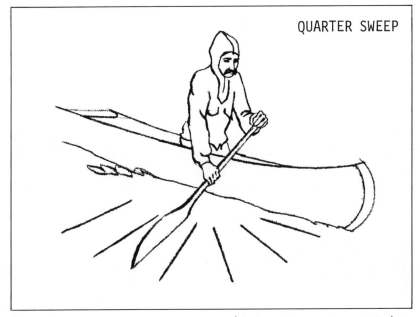

QUARTER SWEEP

(DRAWING BY ROBERT RUSSELL)

canoe you are paddling, and whether you are paddling solo or tandem.

In *all sweeps,* extend the paddle (the blade at right angles to the water), so that when it catches, it is just under the surface of the water. The almost horizontal position of the paddle gives the advantage of an oar swinging in an oarlock. The pulling power of a long sweep in a wide arc quickly brings the canoe about.

Bowman's Sweep Stroke

The bowman executes his quarter sweep stroke (see illustration) by extending the paddle directly ahead as far as he comfortably can. When the blade is just under the surface, he swings it outward and back through a quarter-circle (90°) arc.

This sweep turns the canoe *away from* the side on which the stroke is made. *Caution*: To continue the sweep stroke beyond a point directly opposite the paddler (to make an arc larger than a one-quarter circle) is to nullify the turning action of the canoe.

Of course, there may be some unusual circumstance under which a nullifying action would be needed, such as when a decision to sweep and turn proves immediately to be in error and needs such action if expedient.

65

Recovery for the bowman's sweep stroke is the same as for the basic bow cruising stroke. "Feather" the paddle blade, return to the starting point directly ahead if you want to turn farther, dip, "catch," and sweep again.

"Feather" the blade regardless of the next type of stroke that wind-water conditions require.

Reverse Sweep Stroke

The bowman's sweep stroke discussed above can be executed in the opposite way to secure opposite movement by the canoe. This reverse sweep stroke action is from abeam to bow. It turns the canoe in the direction of the side on which the stroke is made.

Catching the water directly abeam, the paddler sweeps the blade forward in a quarter-circle arc (90°) until the paddle is on a line straight ahead of the bow.

Tandem Sweep Strokes

In tandem canoeing (two paddlers), when the bowman executes a straight sweep stroke on one side, the sternman executes a reverse sweep on the opposite side.

The sternman dips his paddle astern in almost horizontal position and sweeps the paddle forward through a 90° arc (one-quarter of a circle) to a point directly abeam.

It is easy to understand that the bowman is sweeping a straight stroke on one side of the canoe to turn it to the opposite side, on which opposite side the sternman is executing a reverse sweep to turn the canoe toward the side on which he is paddling.

In principle, this is no different from the basic cruising situation in which the bowman executes straight cruising strokes which tend to turn the canoe slightly in the direction away from the stroke while the sternman executes the J stroke on the opposite side to keep the canoe on a straight course.

Pivoting a Canoe

When the bowman executes straight sweep strokes on one side while the sternman simultaneously executes reverse sweep strokes on the other, tandem paddlers can pivot a canoe within an area of water approximately no larger in diameter than the length of the canoe. Or,

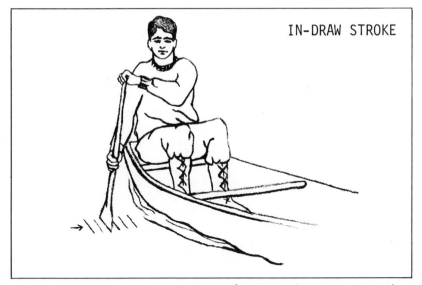

IN-DRAW STROKE

(DRAWING BY ROBERT RUSSELL)

tandem paddlers can (with practice) pivot a canoe within any portion of a circle they decide on in advance.

Solo Sweep

In solo canoeing, with the paddler in the center of a stationary canoe, a full sweep of the paddle in a 180° arc on one side of the canoe, followed by a full 180° reverse sweep on the opposite side, will sharply spin the craft.

Paddle Wide

Many times, in a wind and/or strong current, a substitute for the sweep stroke can be used to keep a canoe on course. The bowman can resort to "paddling wide," a regular, basic bow cruising stroke, with one vital difference: the blade enters the water about a foot or more *away* from the side of the canoe. That action continues with a modified sweep stroke, then finishes in the regular bow-stroke pattern along the side of the canoe.

The sternman, too, paddles wide, on the side of the canoe opposite the bowman, gaining the advantage of a sweep stroke without sacrificing forward progress.

67

DRAW AND PUSHOVER STROKES

The most simple, and probably the most useful, strokes are the draw strokes and their opposite, the pushover strokes. The strokes offer good control for getting around obstructions and in docking.

Draw Stroke

Execute the draw stroke by reaching well out at a right angle to the canoe, with the face of the blade toward the canoe and paddler. With the lower arm in a lever action on a vertical paddle, pull! This stroke pulls the canoe laterally (sideways) to the point of draw.

Make the recovery by quickly turning the blade edgewise to the canoe at the end of the pull. In vertical position, push the paddle through the water to a point at arm's length. Again face the blade toward the canoe, and pull inward.

If cruising at good speed, however, make the recovery from this stroke by quickly slicing the paddle out of the water, in order to prevent it from being forced under the canoe.

In varied executions of the draw stroke, the blade can be pulled in at various angles to effect differences in direction. Only experimentation will determine the effect of modified angles in various pulls.

Move Sideways or Pivot

The draw stroke executed on the same side by both bowman and sternman will move the canoe sideways. To pivot, the bowman executes the stroke on the port side, the sternman on the opposite side.

Pushover Stroke

The pushover is the direct opposite of the draw stroke. Place the blade against the side of the canoe, and push out with the lower arm, driving the canoe away from the paddling side.

The pushover stroke is not so powerful as the straight draw (discussed above); but many times, because of rocks, weeds, or shallow water, to execute the draw stroke on the opposite side may be impractical.

68

JAM STROKE

(DRAWING BY ROBERT RUSSELL)

Right-Angle Turn

You can have the canoe make a right-angle turn by executing a pushover stroke at the bow and a draw stroke at the stern, both on the same side of the canoe.

JAM AND BACKWATER STROKES

The jam stroke brakes the forward movement of a canoe. The backwater stroke reverses its motion after the canoe stops moving.

Jam Stroke

Hold the paddle in vertical position at the side of the canoe, with the blade at a right angle to it. Slice the paddle downward into the water. With the thumb of your lower hand, lock the paddle shaft securely against the gunwale, while holding your upper hand firmly over the grip of the shaft.

This brakes the forward motion.

To prevent a spill when the jam stroke is applied while under great

69

momentum, both paddlers (bowman and sternman) should apply the brakes simultaneously (on opposite sides of the canoe) on signal from either paddler. The proper execution of the jam stroke requires teamwork as well as good control and strong arms.

Backwater Stroke

It is logical to consider the backwater stroke immediately after the jam stroke, for back-paddling is possible only after the canoe's forward motion has been stopped.

Although the need for reversing the motion of a canoe seldom arises, a canoeist must be prepared to meet such a need. The stroke can be learned within one or two practice sessions.

To execute a backwater stroke, simply reverse the motion of the basic bow cruising stroke, and the canoe will move backward.

Begin the backwater stroke where you would end the bow cruising stroke, slightly beyond your hip, with the shaft held in a vertical position. With a forward push of your bottom arm and a backward pull of your upper arm, push the blade forward in a curved sweep of a modified J stroke.

Then cut free of the water, "feather" the blade, and repeat the stroke.

STERN RUDDER AND BOW RUDDER STROKES

Stern Rudder

Trailing the paddle astern at the end of a stroke, thus avoiding the labor of a J stroke, is the lazy sternman's way of steering or keeping a canoe on course. Trailing the paddle alongside the stern curve of the canoe impedes the forward motion by its rudder action, but keeps the canoe on course. This maneuver can be excused in conditions of shallow, rocky-bottomed, or weedy water, where the powerful movements of the J stroke could impede the paddle stroke or beach the canoe.

Bow Rudder

The bow rudder is a bold stroke which gets an immediate reaction from the canoe. Use it when the canoe must be turned quickly to avoid an obstruction in the line of travel. The bowman drives his blade on edge into the water ahead at an angle of 30° to 45° from

BOW RUDDER STROKE

(DRAWING BY ROBERT RUSSELL)

STERN RUDDER STROKE

(DRAWING BY ROBERT RUSSELL)

the keel line, and holds it firmly in that position. The water resistance brings the bow about sharply in the direction of the blade, which acts as a rudder, and at the same time breaks the forward momentum.

For added control, the shaft of the paddle should be held firmly against the gunwale and held long enough to move the bow laterally to the proper position to assure that the mid-portion of the canoe clears the obstruction.

The sternman cooperates in bringing his end around by executing a reverse quarter-sweep.

SCULLING STROKE

The sculling stroke, a variation of the straight draw stroke, is better for turning the canoe or moving it laterally. Place the paddle blade in a vertical position in the water at a comfortable distance from the canoe. Move the paddle back and forth (fore and aft) in a path parallel to the canoe. The leading edge of the paddle blade, as it sweeps two or more feet, is turned away from the canoe at an angle that produces a diagonal pressure which moves the canoe sideways. On the return swing, turn the blade sharply in the opposite direction to continue pulling the canoe toward the paddling side. Note: Both the forward and the backward movements of the stroke utilize the same face of the paddle blade.

The reverse of this blade action will move the canoe away from the paddling side.

You can learn the strokes that propel a canoe the same way in which you learn any other muscle-mind coordination skill—through an understanding of the strokes and repeated practice in using them.

It takes time and practice to become an expert paddler, for experience is the best teacher. Knowledge of the response of a canoe to various strokes comes only through practice.

Practicing and perfecting your strokes under various conditions of wind and water should help you to become a finished canoeist.

SCULLING STROKE

(DRAWING BY ROBERT RUSSELL)

73

~~~~~

Transporting and Portaging the Canoe

The streamlined canoe, so efficient in parting the water and permitting it to return to the stern without wake, is an ideal craft for transportation and shipping. The canoe can be transported without difficulty by car, station wagon or trailer, by railway, and by plane.

CAR-TOP TRANSPORTATION

The canoe's contour design prevents wind drag, and when it is carried on top of an automobile, it does not impede speed on the highways.

For short canoe hauls to a local lake or river, some protective material—quilt, padding, rubber mats, etc.—should be placed on top of the car. Turn the canoe upside down, and secure it with rope or straps to the front and rear bumpers. The front and rear tie-lines are of equal importance, for the wind pressure of forward car movement places strain on the front line, and a sudden stop greatly strains the rear line.

Lateral slip should be prevented by roping or strapping tie-lines over the inverted canoe and anchoring them to the roof gutters. The commercial tie-lines of rubber shock-cord, S hooks, and eyebolts, easily secured and untied, are better than the homemade turnbuckle type.

On extended overland hauls, the commercial utility carriers, with rubber vacuum cups, crossbars, and straps, are recommended. On the highway, the driver should constantly check the position of the canoe, and adjust the tie-ropes or straps as needed. Loosening of the ties can be caused by wind pressure and by weather conditions which dry rope and cause it to expand.

Fishermen car-top their canoe at dusk on a Jeep Wagoneer equipped with a canoe car-top carrier. (KAISER JEEP CORP.)

Lifting the Canoe to the Car-Top

For placing the canoe onto the top of a car, the two-man lift is best. The men face each other from the ends of the inverted canoe that is parallel to, and about three feet from, the car. Each man places the hand nearest the car on the gunwale, and places his other hand on top of the inverted bottom to steady the canoe. The men then sidestep toward the car, lift the canoe over the rack, and gently place it on the crossbars. Do not push or slide the canoe along the crossbars. Lift the canoe. Center it fore and aft and abeam on the car-top, then make fast all lines.

The one-man lift requires the man performing it to lift the canoe in a straight upward arm position above his head. He sidesteps toward the car, and lowers the leading gunwale (nearest the car) to the edge of the crossbars and, withdrawing the near hand, brings it to the other gunwale. With both hands, he slowly rocks the canoe over the rails, making certain that the gunwale finish is not scratched on the carrier's crossbars.

The paddles can be lashed to the thwarts of the canoe in transit or carried in the car, whichever is more convenient.

TRANSPORT BY RAILROAD

Many Canadian railway trains will freight your canoe to the watercourse of your choice, dropping off you and your craft anywhere along its line, and picking you up later, at a point near the end of your cruise. Railroad employees, accustomed to hauling such precious cargo as canoes, know and respect the freight, and carefully stow your wilderness craft. They will secure it in a fashion that will prevent jostling, chafing damage. (See Chapter 20.)

BUSH-PLANE TRANSPORT

In rented bush-plane transport, the canoeist has very little responsibility in securing the canoe to the plane's undercarriage. The canoe's streamlined shape makes it possible for the pilot to attach it outside the plane without greatly affecting speed, maneuverability, or safety. The anchoring ties, very tight to the plane, with the topside up toward the belly of the plane, will permit an unbroken flow of wind about it at top speed. In having canoes transported by bush pilots for hundreds of miles, the author has found them to be most competent and safety-conscious, and their reputation guarantees the passenger's ease of mind.

CANOEING IN MANY LANDS

Should the canoeist's fancy lead to visions of far-flung places, there is no need to worry about the availability of canoes. The canoe is enjoyed universally, and rivers of many lands now know the paddle of the canoeist: the Danube, Volga, Vistula, Rhine, and Seine rivers of

Europe; the Amazon, Parana, Plata, Orinoco, and Uruguay rivers of South America; the Rio Grande and Colorado rivers of Mexico; the Thames, Avon, Severn, and Trent rivers in England; and the Mackenzie, Saskatchewan, Snake, Berens, Churchill, and Athabasca rivers of Canada.

The above represent only a partial list of main waterways with canoe cruising potential in those countries. Many smaller rivers also are inviting. For specific information, contact the consular office representing the country of your interest. You will discover that canoes are available, and that water to suit your wants awaits the touch of your paddle.

PORTAGING THE CANOE

"Portage" refers to the extended carry of a canoe across land which connects different bodies of water or drops suddenly to create waterfalls or turbulent rapids. "Carry" generally refers to hauling a canoe over short distances, as from the car or railroad to the water's edge. For purposes of organization, both the long and short carries are herein grouped and discussed together.

After the canoe has been transported to the shore, it will be necessary to carry it properly to the launching site. To take the canoe from the top of the car, first loosen all ties; then reverse the loading procedure, gently setting down the canoe.

The various carries are discussed in detail below.

One-Man Hip Carry

In this simple carry (used for short distances), the canoeist stands alongside and facing the middle-point-of-balance section of the canoe. With both hands, grasp the nearside gunwale and lift the canoe so that its bottom rests against your knees. Bend over, reach across with your right hand to grasp the far side of the center thwart, and roll the canoe upward off the ground so that it rests on your side, nestled just above the hip.

For persons with a short reach, who have difficulty in reaching across to the opposite side of the canoe, the right hand can be crooked under the thwart inside the canoe, while the left grips the gunwale with an inward pull toward the body.

One-Man Overhead Carry

This carry is classic: in romantic picture and story, from the red man to modern man, it symbolizes best the lightness of the canoe as it is carried overland.

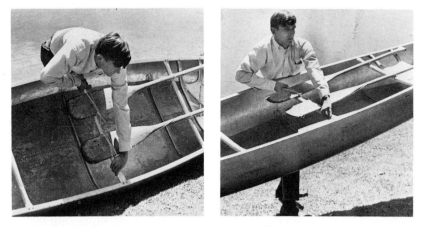

One-Man Hip Carry. *Left*: The canoeist lifts the canoe so that its bottom rests against his knees. Then he bends over and reaches across to grasp the far side of the center thwart. *Right*: He rolls the canoe upward off the ground and rests it to nestle just above his hip, where he can easily carry it to or from the shore. (PHOTOS BY JOE MIGON)

On long portages, the 18-foot and smaller canoes are best carried by one man. Two men have difficulty keeping in step, especially on rocky and hilly portage paths. The undulating terrain and the narrow path cause each carrier to jostle the other fellow's shoulders, and each swears that he is the one who is toting the whole load.

When you are first learning it, the maneuver of getting the canoe up onto your shoulders is quite tricky. The procedure begins as did the one-man hip carry. With your left hand on the near gunwale, nestle the canoe bottom close to your knees, while your right hand tightly grasps the far side of the center thwart. An upward heave of your right arm, with help from a slight boost with one knee, helps the canoe upward as it is rolled close to your body. Then both arms come into play, pushing upward as the canoe is lifted, and you duck your head and twist your shoulders to come up under the overturned canoe. Then gently bring down the canoe to rest on your shoulders under the carrying yoke. Slide your hands forward along the gunwales for a three-point (shoulders and two hands) support of the canoe. Slightly raise the front or leading edge of the canoe for better vision while walking along.

For the single carrier, the "walk up" system is a simpler method of shouldering the canoe. Lift the upsidedown canoe from the bow end, and bring it up to the thigh. Then, with your hands on the gunwales,

One-Man Overhead Carry. The Hip Carry on the opposite page is the starting position for the Overhead Carry. *Left*: The canoeist continues the lift with an upward heave of his arms. A slight boost with one knee helps the canoe upward as it rolls close to his body. *Right*: As the canoe is lifted, the carrier ducks his head and twists his shoulders to come up under the carrying yoke. (PHOTOS BY JOE MIGON)

lift it overhead. Then turn around, so that your back is toward the stern end, which remains on the ground. Under the canoe, back up toward the center, while your hands hold the canoe above your head as they slide along the gunwales. When you reach the center-point-of-balance, the stern end will slowly rise, and once balanced—parallel to the ground—place the canoe on your shoulders for carrying.

According to draft rejection reports, modern men are weak in the shoulder girdle, and the idea of heaving a canoe overhead may seem beyond the strength of most weekend canoeists. This is not true. Along the portage trails of the Superior-Quetico canoe country, the author has seen teen-age girl canoeists hit the beach and unload, and without hesitation, one of them has lifted the canoe to her shoulders. She was off on the portage trek, while the other carried the packsacks—quickly and efficiently—in a manner that bespoke the "veteran," in spite of their young years and seeming lack of muscle.

In the one-man overhead carries, setting down the canoe is simply a matter of getting out from under it and gently laying it down. A slight upward shove, to lift the canoe from the yoke pads, and the head is ducked to the outside (either side). Holding firmly to the gunwales, the carrier brings down the canoe, close to the body, in stages: first, to the thigh; then to the knees; and gently to the ground—very much in reverse procedure to the original shouldering procedure.

Two-Man Shoulder Carry

The lift-and-roll method of raising a canoe in the one-man carry can be used by two men, thereby lessening the load. One man stands at the bow-thwart position to a canoe on the ground; and the other man at the stern-thwart position, as the canoe is brought up and nestled against their knees. With the left hand of both men on the near gunwale, their right hands reach across to the opposite gunwale; and on signal, they lift the canoe with a knee boost, and roll it upside down and overhead as they duck. The canoe comes to rest, with the stern thwart or seat on the shoulder of one carrier, and the bow thwart or seat on the shoulders of the other.

Two-Man Wedge Carry

One of the simplest two-man carries, over short distances, is the wedge carry. The man up front places his hand under the front wedge, or deck, and the stern carrier (on the opposite side) grasps, backhanded, under the stern wedge, as the canoe is carried right side up and parallel to the ground.

Two-Man Gunwale Carry

In this carry, two men stand on either side of the center of the upright canoe. They lean over and grasp with the near hand, and, hooking the fingers under the inwale, lift the balanced canoe, and turn their bodies in the direction of the carry.

This simple carry is ideal for taking the canoe to shore for launching. In fact, regardless of the carry used, it is recommended that canoeists switch to this carry for placing the canoe, stern first, into the water.

At the water's edge, the men slide their hands back along the gunwales, permitting the stern end of the canoe to dip into the water. They then feed the canoe, hand-over-hand, into the water without scraping the dock or any sand or rocks that may injure the bottom of the canoe.

Top: At the University of Miami in Coral Gables, Florida, students Mary Stokes (at the stern) and Vicki Alexander (at the bow) demonstrate the Two-Man Wedge Carry. Before, between, and after classes, students take advantage of the University's canoeing facility sponsored by the Student Union. *Bottom*: Miss Alexander and Miss Stokes execute a Three-Man Wedge Carry with Greg Gacek, who makes an adjustment for his size in the team by carrying the stern with his arms under the keel. (PHOTOS BY JOE MIGON)

Three-Man Wedge Carry

The wedge carry for two can be used by three carriers. The carriers of the same size and strength, probably young people, stand on opposite sides of the bow of the canoe, facing forward. Each grasps the bow edge on his side. The third carrier grasps, back-handed, the stern wedge of the upright canoe.

Three-Man Shoulder Carry

When carried by three men, the canoe also can be shouldered. Two persons of the same size, up front, carry the upside-down canoe with gunwales resting on their shoulders. The lone stern carrier places his shoulder under the deck near the end of the canoe. A padding of clothing on the gunwales and deck increases comfort. This carry is recommended for narrow paths, for it provides good visibility for the carriers.

Four-Man Carries

It is advisable to use as many hands as are practical when portaging the freighter canoes (18 feet and over) on extended trips and when children carry the lighter canoes.

In the four-man carry, two men stand at either side of the bow, and two stand astern of the right-side-up canoe. Each bends over and grasps the nearside gunwale or thwart, whichever is best for balance; then all lift the canoe and carry it right side up.

Light duffle and delicate gear may be left in the canoe. This is a simple, nonphotogenic, unglamorous carry, but when the footing is adequate, this carry saves strain. Should the terrain be rocky or stumpy, use this carry, but invert the canoe to eliminate the danger of bumping and scuffing its bottom.

In the case of a narrow, winding, and brushy path, the four men can shoulder the canoe in the same fashion as in the three-man shoulder carry.

Top: Three-Man Shoulder Carry demonstrated by Roger Beasley, Greg Gacek, and the author at the stern. *Bottom*: Right-Side-Up Four-Man Wedge Carry demonstrated by Greg Gacek and Roger Beasley grasping the stern wedge, and Vicki Alexander and Mary Stokes grasping the bow wedge. (PHOTOS BY JOE MIGON)

83

Yokes

In all one-man carries, use a yoke to cushion the weight of the canoe on the shoulders. Always place the yoke amidships, at the point-of-balance.

Yokes come in three different forms:

1) Most modern canoes have a pair of built-in padded cushions, properly angled and anchored to the center thwart. They are sturdy oblong frames, sufficiently padded, and they do not interfere with the design or function of the canoe.

2) The clamp style of yoke is like a thwart, bowed at the center, with a padded surface on the sides of the curve that fit around the neck-rests on the shoulders. A bolt and wingnut assembly at the ends of the hardwood arm enables the canoeist to clamp it to the gunwales at the center-of-balance point. After one portage has been completed, and there are no others in sight, unscrew the yoke and place it in the bottom of the canoe.

3) Canoe paddles also can be used as carrying yokes. If you do not have a detachable or built-in yoke, improvise one. Lash two paddles to the thwarts, at a slight V angle. Lash the shafts (near the grip end) of the paddles to the bow thwart. Position the blades at an angle so that you will have flat surfaces for each shoulder and close to your neck. Tie the paddles securely with leather thongs, light line, or straps, for much stress is placed on this improvised yoke. Pad the blade surfaces with a shirt or sweater for comfortable carrying.

The canoe is most vulnerable to injury when it is out of its natural element. In transportation and portaging, exercise utmost care!

The various methods of carrying your canoe are discussed above: (1) to encourage you to use as many hands as possible to ease the load; (2) to insure adequate out-of-water canoe protection; (3) to provide maximum safety for the carriers.

10

Launch, Load, Board, and Cast Off!

The respect and care that in the preceding chapters you have been encouraged to accord your canoe should continue to be basic in launching, loading, and boarding your craft. Unloaded, the canoe is light enough to be launched easily and properly by one or two persons. Once it is ready for launching, always carry it to the water. Never drag, pull, push, or slide along your canoe!

LAUNCHING

The carries in which the canoe is handled right side up (discussed in the preceding chapter) are ideal for launching purposes: (1) one-man hip, and (2) two-man gunwale.

One-Man Hip Launch

From the hip-carry approach, a solo canoeist can walk to the water's edge, lower the leading edge of the canoe into the water, then float or feed it along by running the hands back toward shore on the near-side gunwale, as the canoe slides across the thigh.

Holding one gunwale will tilt the canoe as you feed it into the water, stern first. You can right the canoe after it becomes completely waterborne. Bring the canoe around to a parallel-to-shore position by gunwale or line manipulation. Then board the canoe amidship by bending low, putting one foot into the center, grasping both gunwales, and bringing your other foot into the canoe. Then work your way to your position.

Place the paddle in the canoe before boarding, or take it in during the boarding procedure.

Variation: One man can also launch his canoe parallel to the shore (alongside docking) from a dock, high bank, or rocky ledge. Grip the near-side gunwale amidship, and raise the canoe to your knees, then lower it into the water. Extend your toes slightly over the docking edge, and with a slight bend of your knees, extend the canoe out over the water and allow it to ease down into the water. Your toes should keep the canoe bottom from scraping the docking edge.

DOCK LAUNCH

Two-Man Gunwale Beach Launch

This beach launching technique begins with two men standing amidship on opposite sides, holding the gunwales and walking side-step up to the water's edge. They gently lower the stern end first into the water. Once the stern is afloat, they feed the canoe hand-over-hand into the water, at right angles to the shore. When the canoe is completely afloat (except possibly for the bow end, barely touching the sand bottom), the bowman steadies the canoe by bracing it between his knees, in a straddling position, then for additional support leans over and places his hands on the gunwales.

86

Top: Greg Gacek illustrates the ease of handling a canoe from the hip position. This simple skill makes it easy to launch the craft or carry it from the water. *Bottom:* Mary Stokes and Vicki Alexander use a Two-Man Gunwale Carry to launch their canoe. (PHOTOS BY JOE MIGON)

Dock, Bank, and Ledge Launches (Alongside Docking)

The two-man, hand-over-hand, launch—feeding the canoe into the water by the gunwales—can also be used when launching from a dock, high bank, or rocky ledge.

The advantages that accrue from this possibility are that the canoe *can* be brought parallel to the shore for handy loading and for easier passenger boarding. These advantages are gained only when certain principles are followed. The bowman squats near the edge of the dock, facing the canoe's bow. The step to the center of the canoe is with a downward pressure—not lateral which would tend to push the canoe away—then he bends over, grasps the gunwales with both hands and brings his other foot from the dock and places it beside the first. He then takes paddling position, and the advantage is won.

The sternman enters the same way, and moves to his position.

Should there be a third person, for stabilizing purposes (weight in the center), he is the first to board.

BOARDING FROM BEACH

The sternman steps around his partner who is straddling the bow, places one foot on the bottom of the canoe, grasps the gunwales, and brings in his other foot. With toes slightly turned in and with both hands on the gunwales, sliding them along to keep his body low as he progresses, he moves to the stern end of the canoe.

Usually the sternman places the paddle in the canoe before he boards, but he may hold it across the gunwales and slide it along as he proceeds forward. Once in position with his paddle in the water, the sternman stabilizes the craft for the bowman's entry.

The bowman lifts the canoe forward, free of the bottom, and with a slight push-off, enters. He steps directly into the canoe or kneels on the deck, then steps in. Once aboard, in order to prevent the bottom of the canoe from scraping, he may find it necessary (it frequently is) to proceed amidships as the sternman maneuvers the canoe into deeper water. Only when the canoe is sufficiently afloat does the bowman return to his paddling position. To proceed lakeward, it is necessary to turn the canoe around, as the bow is shoreward.

Some canoeists claim that the bow should enter the water first, in which case the partners' procedures of boarding are reversed—the bowman enters first, etc. It seems more logical to launch stern first, because in proper canoe trim, the bow is slightly higher.

LANDING

For landing, the launching procedure is reversed. The bowman disembarks first, and steadies the canoe with knees and hands. Then the sternman comes forward.

For brief stops, both men pull up the canoe, hand-over-hand, until it is balanced amidships. Then both carry it a short distance from the water.

For long periods of rest and at campsites, the canoe should be carried well back from the water's edge and turned upside down. High winds and waves, which develop all too suddenly, can pound and damage a canoe that remains partially in the water. Also, there is the danger of its being blown adrift—it has happened!

In landing situations, never pull the bow of a canoe out of the water with the keel angled on a solid surface (dock or ledge). The angled keel will, in effect, make the canoe a tightrope, and the chances are great for upsetting the sternman and duffle.

LOADING: SOME BASIC PRINCIPLES OF BALANCE

A few simple experiments illustrate the basic principles of canoe stability in loading—principles which also have validity in all cruising situations. Perform these drills in shallow water, preferably with you and your partner in swimming trunks.

You remain in the canoe, while your partner stands alongside at the amidships position.

1) Sit on the middle thwart, then shift position to either side—port or starboard.

2) Stand up in the middle of the canoe, then step to either side as far as possible.

3) Sit in a regular paddling position. Then tell your partner to exert downward pressure on one gunwale.

In each of the above situations, experiments designed to illustrate the principle of the center of gravity, the canoe will lurch and probably dislodge the passenger.

The "center of gravity" is a point around which the whole mass of an object can be balanced. The farther from that point of balance (center of gravity), the more unstable is the equilibrium of a canoe or any other object. When a canoe is afloat, the lifting force of the water under it is called "buoyancy." The floating hull, with the upward pressure of water below it, resists weight (passengers and cargo):

therefore, the weight must be centrally disposed around a single point of balance to maintain upright stability.

A floating craft also has a "center of buoyancy," that must be aligned with the center of gravity to insure equilibrium of the craft and stability under way.

The canoe has no heavy keel or built-in ballast as have larger boats. It must establish its own center of buoyancy from the weight of the occupants and all additional freight.

The stability of the canoe comes from the ballast being disposed as low as possible. In truth, a loaded canoe—within its prescribed weight limits—is more stable than an empty one; that is, the center of gravity is lower.

In alongside loading (from a dock, high bank, or rocky shelf) where the canoe is parallel to the shore, the chore of stowing duffle is facilitated. The entire inside area of the canoe is exposed, and the solid footing is an advantage. While one canoeist steadies the canoe by holding the near-side gunwale, his partner stows the duffle in position.

In loading a canoe from a beach or in shallow water, use the following procedure: stack all equipment on the water's edge, within reach of the bowman, who uses his knees to straddle the canoe whose bow end is slightly out of the water. The sternman steps around the bowman, boarding as explained earlier, turns around toward the bowman and receives from him the duffle as it is passed. The sternman stows each pack for proper balance. If necessary for safety, he lashes non-floating duffle bags to thwarts.

Some Principles of Loading for Safety in Cruising

1) Place the heaviest duffle as close as possible to the bottom of the canoe.

2) If you expect to encounter water spray from high waves, it is advisable slightly to raise the duffle from the bottom of the canoe. Place a light mat of spruce boughs on the bottom of the canoe—or use a packboard which has a two-inch wooden frame all around it.

3) Place all lighter equipment, such as clothing and bedding, on top of the heavy cargo.

4) Lash all non-buoyant hardware to the thwarts.

5) Keep the maps, compass, rain gear, camera, and binoculars within arm's reach at all times.

6) Securely wedge, beside the duffle or at the bottom where they won't fall overboard when the canoe lurches, the extra paddle, fishing

PRINCIPLES OF CANOE LOADING

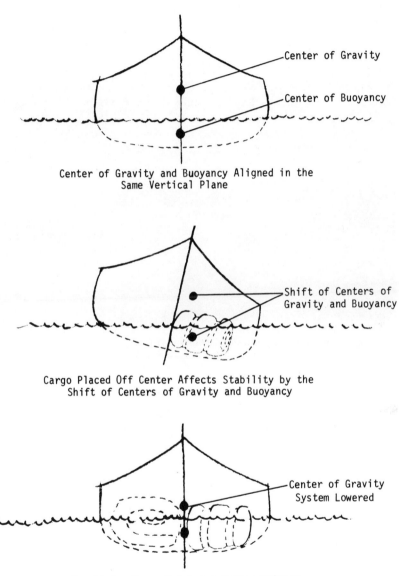

Center of Gravity and Buoyancy Aligned in the
Same Vertical Plane

Cargo Placed Off Center Affects Stability by the
Shift of Centers of Gravity and Buoyancy

Equalizing Cargo Maintains Proper Balance

(DRAWINGS BY ROBERT RUSSELL)

91

rods, and the axe (preferably tied together in one bundle).

7) When you transport packs with metal frames, packboards with wooden frames, or boxes with sharp corners, take precautions to prevent their hard surfaces from rubbing the ribs or the planking of the canoe.

Cruising in an 18-foot Guide's Special, with the canoe properly loaded and principles of balance observed, the craft rides with the bow slightly higher than the stern. (OLD TOWN CANOE CO.)

8) Arrange and rearrange duffle by shifting the packs until proper trim is achieved. (With experience, efficient loading of a canoe will "come naturally.")

9) Trim, as it relates to proper loading, must be considered in two ways: (*a*) fore and aft; and (*b*) from side to side. This can be determined only after all paddlers and passengers and the full load of gear are aboard.

10) Under way, the bow of a loaded canoe should ride a trifle higher than the stern.

After the duffle is loaded, secured, and covered, the sternman moves to his position, and, with his paddle in the water, steadies the canoe. He then gives the signal for the push-off!

Your canoe, properly trimmed and balanced according to the principles discussed, will perform efficiently—even though unexpected situations (a sudden gust of wind, scraping on an underwater boulder, strong currents, or high waves) develop to affect its center of gravity. The canoe will recover immediately and right itself for continuing safe travel.

11

Outboarding, Sailing,
Rowing, Poling

The canoe, increasingly popular on the States and Canadian pleasure-craft scene, is versatile. In addition to being propelled by paddle, your canoe can be powered with a small outboard motor; it can also be sailed, rowed, or poled.

OUTBOARDING

To paddle to remote areas by way of large lakes and swift rivers, and to carry the canoe across numerous portages, requires strength, stamina, and a good deal of available time. Many modern canoeists are not conditioned physically, nor do they have the time, to travel by muscle power (paddling) alone. The use of a small outboard motor (1 to 3 horsepower) to push along the canoe is the answer. Canoe manufacturers, aware of the popularity of the outboard motor, have added the square-stern model, in many sizes, to enable one to attach the motor efficiently. American- and European-made motors, efficient, light, economical in the use of fuel, with little flash or gadgetry, cruise for more than five hours on one gallon of gas.

The type of water, the number of portage carries, and the size of the canoe will determine the horsepower and weight of the motor. The canoeist should keep in mind that a heavy motor on a small canoe will adversely affect its trim, balance, freeboard, etc.

Should you decide to use a motor, add sheer pins, extra spark plugs, and cotter pins to your tool kit.

Enjoying a 16-foot square-stern canoe built for use with an outboard. Center length is 15 feet, 11 inches; gunwale length is 16 feet, 2 inches; maximum depth is 15 inches, with a 35-inch beam. The craft is built with .050 gauge aluminum and weighs approximately 80 pounds. (RICHLAND MFG. CO.)

As "going light" is of constant concern in tripping, the majority of participants in the trip must make the final decision about the practicability of using an outboard.

The canoeing purists reject the use of such a modern convenience as the outboard, citing the encumbrance on portage trails, the weight of metal and gasoline, the smell, and the noise.

Users of the outboard claim that they are more realistic. With the wide range of canoe routes available, they simply do not include in their itinerary those with numerous rapids requiring portages. The outboard quickly takes the canoeists away from civilization, then the paddlers can take over. The motor is welcome in backtracking a route, in meeting the requirements of a pick-up schedule, and in situations that may call for fast emergency travel.

In regular cruising situations, speed should rarely be the sole justification for the outboard. For more economical use of fuel, observation advantages, and safety factors, the motor should rarely be driven "wide open."

The skier uses chair lifts and T bars to carry him to the top of the slope, so that he has more time and energy to enjoy the exhilarating runs down. So, too, the canoeist, from the very young to the aged, has more time for multiple pleasures with motor power. The average canoeist will cover about 18 miles in a day of paddling, while a 3-horsepower outboard, averaging 6 m.p.h., will take a canoe the same distance in three hours.

A combination of outboarding and paddling offers an ideal arrangement. With less energy and time expended in paddling, one has more opportunity for setting up a comfortable camp in a proper setting, more time for fishing, rock-hounding, exploring, prospecting, and photographing.

In quiet bays, along scenic stretches of water, and on mirror calms, it would seem sacrilegious to use the silence-breaking noise of an outboard. The peaceful stretches of water, the calm of morning and evening hours, silently ask the paddler to fit the mood. The noise of an outboard is quite admissible on a large lake while the wind is roaring and the waves are billowing and splashing. Canoeists, who are lovers of the outdoors, will understand when to paddle, when to use the outboard.

Some state and national parks ban outboards because their noise can disturb wild animals and birds and their wakes can disturb aquatic life. Always check in advance with the park whether or not an outboard may be used, and what limit is placed on its size.

SAILING

Sailing adds another dimension to your canoeing adventure. Your canoe is the cheapest sailboat afloat; few craft are cheaper to own, easier to rig, faster to sail. The canoe sailing rig can be raised or dismantled in minutes, and if water is anywhere close to your home, you can car-top your canoe and go sailing at any time of day or evening.

This discussion of canoe sailing is limited to the canoe-cruising fan who is interested in extending his experiences by adding a small sail for auxiliary and fast (if the wind is right) propulsion. Comment will be confined to the 17- and 18-foot (paddle-steered) canoe with a

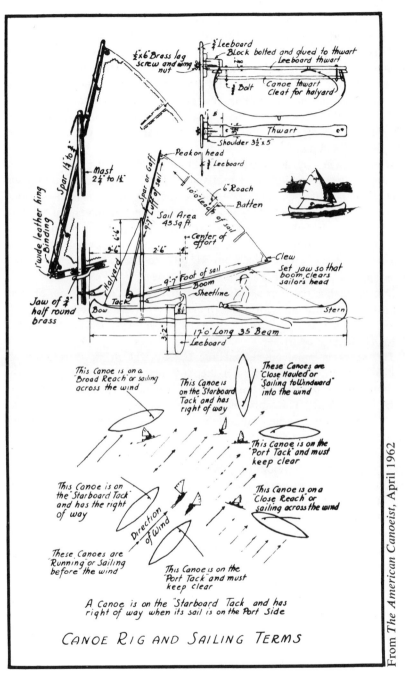

CANOE RIG AND SAILING TERMS

lateen-type sail with a 45-square-foot area, which has proved, over the years, to be ideal for the canoeing recreationist. The lateen sail consists of a nearly equilateral triangular cloth attached to two spars linked together at a meeting point forward of the mast. This rig is the most popular in the United States, and its canvas and rigging necessities are standard equipment among the major canoe manufacturers.

Should the canoeist aspire to extend his range of sailing experience, participate in competitions, etc., there are available progressively more complicated sailing styles.

Whether you buy a sailing rig or build your own depends on time, economy, and your skill as a craftsman. The major canoe companies have "tailor-made" sailing accessories that fit their canoes—wood-canvas, aluminum, fiberglas—and all require their adapters, clips, wing nuts, clamps, drilled holes, etc., engineered for quick attachment and detachment. Without these standard rigs, it will be necessary to adapt a commercial rig, which sells from $150.00 to $250.00, to your canoe. Handymen can make their own for much less.

Dacron makes the best sailcloth, with nylon a second choice. Should you use the traditional cotton sail, make sure it's the fine-spun, 4-ounce grade. The sail is laced to the spars through brass grommets spaced 8 to 10 inches apart.

The spars in a lateen rig include the upright mast. It is about 5 feet 6 inches long, fitted into a step of metal or wood permanently anchored to the bottom of the canoe, up through a special bow thwart, with a mast hole. The horizontal spar is the boom, and the slanting spar is the gaff. Today, aluminum largely replaces the traditional straight-grained spruce spars.

The gaff and boom spars may be joined by using two large screw-eyes and a brass S hook or a strip of heavy leather. The jaw for holding the boom close to the mast (see diagram) is best made from 3/4 inch half-round brass, and fastened to the boom about 13 to 18 inches from the forward end.

In rigging, the best materials for the halyard—for hoisting the sail on the mast—are the modern synthetic lines, such as braided nylon or dacron, which glide through pulleys as if greased, and which do not rot. Jam-free pulleys with nylon rollers are preferred, and cleats may be made of anything from wood to plastics, as long as they are strong enough. The main sheet—the line that controls the sail—should be diamond-braided 1/4-inch polyethylene line, which will float if dropped overboard.

The leeboard is a substitute for the keel, and prevents the canoe, while sailing, from sliding sidewise in the water. The leeboard, attached to a cross-member support, is rigidly fastened with J hooks to the gunwales, and placed approximately 2½ feet astern of the mast. The leeboard, hanging in the water, should pivot freely to enable it to swing up when beaching the canoe, while cruising in shallow or rock strewn water, or while sailing a downwind course.

An Old Town Moliter Canoe Rigged with a Class "C" Sail (OLD TOWN CANOE CO.)

When you use a supplier's standard sailing unit, the adaptations of stepping the mast and proper hanging of the leeboard are so located that you can sail with little strain on the steering paddle. Therefore, you will be getting the most speed from the craft.

In solo sailing, small bags of sand ballast are helpful in achieving proper trim. The canoe under sail will run well, point high on windward course, come about easily. It serves as its own life preserver, for it stays afloat even when swamped.

For your first experience in sailing, select a wide stretch of water, without dangerous currents or obstructions, and not too subject to squalls. (Lakes surrounded by trees and high bluffs, and with many islands, are apt to be squally.) When your canoe is properly rigged, push off lakeward, drop the leeboard, and hoist your sail. As the sail catches the wind and fills, slack off your mainsail a little, keeping the rope in your hand until you find the right angle (in the neighborhood of 45°) for increasing speed. You can hold the canoe down by lying on a gunwale if necessary. Stay low to decrease wind resistance.

Canoe sailing is as old as the canoe itself. Modern Cree Indians in Canada still use the traditional methods of their forefathers to ease the chore of paddling. Whenever the course is downwind, they push their paddle shafts through the sleeves of jackets or shirts, and, from the bow position, spread apart the paddles to catch the wind in a primitive but useful sail. The lateen sailing rig is a bit more sophisticated and represents a modern first step to the adventure of riding the wind.

Information on canoe sailing rigs is available from the major canoe companies, and from Bruce Clark, 115 McGavrock Pike, Nashville, Tenn. 37214, the local American Red Cross chapter, Boy Scouts of America, the Sailing Editor of the *American Canoist Magazine* (Roger Wilkinson, Oak Tree Lane, Rumson, N.J. 07760), the Chicagoland Canoe Base, 4019 N. Narragansett Ave., Chicago, Ill. 60634, and Western-Hoege Co., 915 S. Grand Ave., Los Angeles, Calif. 90015.

ROWING

The canoe makes an excellent rowing craft when equipped with the attachments of oarlock arms, sliding seat, adjustable foot stretchers, and spoon-blade racing oars. The rowing rig is easily attached to a canoe by means of four clamps with wing nuts. No tools are needed, and installation time is about a minute. The rig combines the maneuverability and carrying capacity of a rowboat and some of the speed of a racing shell.

Summer camp directors report that older boys and girls are especially partial to the competitive factor generated by the new style (for the canoe) of propulsion power. The rowing rigs also give novices confidence in canoe-handling. Their durability makes them feasible in enabling campers to get racing-shell experience without going to the expense of buying a real shell—which would be too delicate for rough use.

According to claims of the Canoe-Swift rowing rig kit (Grumman Boats), the canoe can be converted into a racing shell, a young person's rowing trainer, a high-speed life-saving or emergency craft, and a fast heavy-duty boat for camping.

The combination of racing oars and sliding seat moves the canoe much faster than paddling does. The oars are true racing sculls, and the beginner must learn to feather them and to use his legs for propulsion. The thrill of high-speed rowing and the satisfaction of learning to row in college-style crew racing is possible with the rowing rig.

A sliding rowing seat has been attached to this 16-foot fiberglas canoe. The canoeist is using sculling oars. (OLD TOWN CANOE CO.)

POLING

Another aspect of the canoeman's art is poling, essentially both a braking and a propulsion technique, that serves better than paddling in certain situations.

The pole, as a piece of equipment, is rarely carried in the canoe, but is picked up as needed. It should be 10 to 12 feet long and approximately 1½ inches in diameter. It should be shod with an iron spike, attached by means of a cap fitting over the end of the pole and anchored with a nail or a screw. The spike should be detachable, so that it may be carried in a pack and shod to a pole when necessary. Spruce and birch are the best pole materials. The pole should be trimmed and smoothed to safeguard your hands.

The only time the canoeist should stand in a canoe is when he is using the pole. The technique of poling is a matter of natural movements which offer little difficulty. After ten minutes' practice, you will learn much about bodily balance and canoe response. Stand forward of the stern seat with your feet apart in good stance, the left foot forward of the right, both toed in, so that (as a right-handed canoeist) you're facing and leaning slightly to the starboard poling side. It is important to be loose, with knees bent so that the forward movement of the canoe will not affect your balance.

For starboard poling, hold the pole with your left hand as near the top as the depth of water permits. Hold the right hand about two feet lower. Then thrust the shod end of the pole slightly forward to the bottom of the water for suitable purchase or bite. Both hands, arms, and shoulders push against the pole, keeping it out about six inches or more from the gunwale.

As the canoe is driven forward, work your hands up the pole, hand-over-hand, as if climbing a rope. Note: Some polers slide both hands along instead of using the hand-over-hand method. To remain in standing position while the canoe moves under you requires a sense of balance. Be careful not to push the canoe out from under you.

Steering (staying on course) is effected by moving the upper hand outward as in a pushover paddle draw stroke, turning the canoe away from the poling side; moving the upper hand as in a pull-over draw stroke turns the canoe toward the poling side. After each thrust, check the course of the canoe. If it is veering too much, don't attempt the next thrust; instead, turn the canoe while the pole is still in the water.

For the next forward thrust, bring the pole out of the water, snap it forward sharply, and make another firm purchase on the bottom. Work only from one side of the canoe. Soon you will learn that presenting the pole into the water at different angles determines various canoe responses.

For deep-water work, poles up to 14 feet are used—mostly by veteran canoeists in specialized activities like freighting, etc.

Select a shallow, quiet section of water for your initial attempts in poling, then work up to a shallow stream where you have boulders, sandbars, and a current to contend with.

Tandem Poling

When there are two polers in a canoe, they work alternately, from bow and stern positions. One pole is always in the water for continuing control—as the canoe loses speed from the first poler's thrust, the other sets his pole to make his move. Unlike paddling, in tandem poling both men pole on the same side of the canoe. Two men can pole from a sitting position when proper current conditions prevail.

Also, the bowman can use his paddle in conventional stroking, steering around obstructions, as the sternman uses the pole.

Two-man poling has real value for upstream work, and veteran poling teams use the pole for downstream running of rapids. In the powerful surge of water in rapids, there is no other way to make progress. The average paddler cannot offset a five-mile-an-hour current, but the pole makes it possible. The many swift and rock-strewn rivers running into Hudson's Bay (Canada) seem impossible to navigate, but veteran canoeists, by poling, conquer them with comparative ease.

In poling, it is basic to keep the canoe headed straight into the current. If the surge of water is allowed to turn the canoe, the current will turn the canoe broadside and defy control.

In traveling downstream rapids, which is more tricky than going up, the canoe should be bow heavy. The advantage of poling downstream is tied up with poling's braking power, where the pole can be used as a drag and a rudder. The stern pole, slanting backward, drags the bottom, serving as a brake and holding the canoe in place momentarily, until the poler figures out his strategy.

Another way of slowing and controlling the canoe in swift water is by "snubbing." In snubbing a canoe, the bowman uses the paddle as needed, while the sternman uses the pole, jabbing it forward about 45° into the stream bottom to check the speed of the canoe. If the canoe begins to turn, the pole is released until proper course is recovered by letting the canoe run a short distance; then with the paddler's help, the sternman snubs again. The procedure will ease the canoe down the turbulence at a safe speed. Snubbing is difficult in very fast waters, and, in such stretches, the dragging method should be used.

At the opposite extreme of poling, I once observed, in a shallow bayou of upper Hamlin Lake, Michigan, an expert canoeist pole his craft in and out of lily-pad cover and across water only four inches deep. He was casting for bass and covered the open spots in far recesses of the bayou. He caught several lunker bass, because, I thought, he was able to cover undisturbed water. The poler's rhythmic grace of movement, the silent propulsion of his craft, were a joy to watch.

Should poling inspire you to a high degree of proficiency, consider the National Poling Event, which is held annually. You may also gain courage from the fact that Ron Kloepper, after but two months of engaging in the sport, won the United States poling championship in 1966.

12

Accessories for Your Canoe

"Sunday" canoeing has many adherents who enjoy its relaxation, as did their forebears at the turn of the century, when every town adjacent to water could boast of one or more canoe clubs.

With accessories, you can outfit your canoe as a luxury craft, suitable for inviting your most comfort- and civilization-oriented friend for a cruise around the local lagoon or on some nearby gently flowing water.

Seats and Cushions. The crew seat enables the non-paddling passenger to sit a few inches above the floor of the canoe. Foldable when not in use, the crew seat of canvas over a frame of aluminum tubing, with rubber-tipped legs (that prevent sliding), is an ideal accessory. Also available are sturdy, comfortable folding slat and folding cane chairs. Without a chair, the passenger can sit on a cushion, facing the paddler, and lean against a slat back rest that is placed against the bow thwart. Life-preserver type cushions have floating in addition to comfort value. Available for the paddler is a canoe-seat cushion of foam, encased in durable vinyl, that straps under the canoe-seat frame.

Floor Mats. For recreational canoeing, you should protect the floor of your canoe against moisture, which causes slippery footing. The wood slat or rolamat floor protection can be used to good advantage. One type consists of long-grained hardwood cross slats, thoroughly seasoned and chemically treated to prevent rotting and warping, joined together by galvanized rust-proof connectors, or hinges, that permit roll-up storage. Another type of canoe-bottom passenger protection consists of wood-slat floorboards that run longitudinally the length of the canoe floor. The openings between strips permit feet and gear to remain dry.

Bow and Stern Handles. For the two-man canoe carry and for the attachment of lines to your canoe, sturdy, ornate handles can be screwed to the bow and stern decks.

Bailer. Shipped water (from leaks or high waves) that accumulates in the bottom of the canoe must be bailed out to prevent the soaking of duffle and the feet of passengers. There are several types of plastic detergent bottles with recessed handles that make ideal bailers. Replace the cap, but cut off the bottom of the bottle at the angle of a scoop. Stow the bailer in the stern end of the canoe, as the forward movement and the trim of a canoe under way sends the water sternward. For small volumes of water, use a large cellulose sponge, which can also be used as a wiper to remove accumulated mud and debris.

Lines. A 30- to 50-foot line or painter should be attached to both the bow and stern ends for tying to a dock, towing, and tracking a canoe. Manila rope, 3/8 inch in diameter, is generally used, but the synthetics—dacron, nylon, polyethylene—are stronger, water-, fungus-, and mildew-proof, and they will outlast all other ropes. The synthetic ropes are expensive. When you use them, double-check their knots, as their hard, slick texture causes knots to slip. Keep your lines coiled and dry when not in use.

Canoe Car-top Carrier. The light weight of a canoe makes it easy to car-top. In high-speed automobile travel, it is of utmost importance that the carrier be solidly attached to the car and the canoe to the carrier. The crossbars, in oak or aluminum, with heavy-duty suction cups and attaching straps (to rain gutter of car), keep the canoe from sliding or slipping. Some crossbars come with canvas-covered foam cushions to protect the gunwales from scraping. Also available are bars of aluminum that extend to 76-inch width, suitable for transporting two canoes.

Canoe Tie-Downs. Instead of rope, use straps over the canoe that are made from heavy-duty, 1-inch webbing, with spring-loaded, plated buckles. Polyethylene rope or rubber straps with S hook fittings are used to tie the bow and stern ends to the car bumpers.

Outboard Motor Bracket. Powering a double-end canoe with a motor requires the mounting of a side bracket anchored to the gunwales behind the stern seat and extending over the port side of the canoe. The bracket can be of oak and reinforced plywood, but aluminum is most frequently used. Brackets are easy and quick to mount, adjustable to fit all double-end models, require no structural changes, and will hold up to a 4-horsepower motor.

Portage Yoke. The modern portage yoke consists of two padded cushions, angled slightly, secured to a varnished oak or aluminum crossbar with fasteners that are clamped amidships at the point of balance. Remove the yoke assembly if you wish, or let it remain anchored to the canoe. Many canoe designs include yoke pads permanently affixed to the center thwart that seem not to interfere with gear storage or the comfort of a third passenger. Pads are available that can be attached to paddles lashed to thwarts, to form a carrying yoke.

Pontoons. A canoe can be as stable as a johnboat if a pair of pontoons are rigged outboard of both gunwales to give the craft an ocean-going stability. For as long as men can recall, the stability of the canoe has come from its beam as well as from its length. Pontoons add a stabilizing beam dimension to a canoe.

One type of pontoon is made of Ethafoam, a buoyant plastic unaffected by oils produced by The Dow Chemical Co. Each pontoon, measuring 6 inches in diameter by 60 inches in length, is capable of displacing 57 pounds. Another type of pontoon is called the Piedmont Pontoon, a hollow tube of welded, heavy-gauge aluminum, 7 inches in diameter, 51 inches long, and 16 pounds in weight.

Pontoons can be attached to any canoe by crossarms made of 3/4-inch aluminum pipe which is secured to the gunwales with wing nuts and special clamps. On newer models of canoes, there is no need to drill a hole to attach pontoons, and, when pontoons are removed, the canoe returns to its original form.

While cruising, the canoe moves as if it had no pontoons, for, except when the canoe is tipped, they do not touch the water. The forward ends of the pontoons are slanted, so that they will slice through the water with the least possible resistance and splash.

When pontoons are used for added safety, certain features of the streamlined virtues of a canoe are lost. In addition to sacrificing speed, pontoons can cause splash and spray. Paddling is more difficult, and progress is noisier in choppy water.

The canoeist who uses his craft for hunting and fishing, who criss-crosses large bodies of water hauling large cargoes, etc., should think of pontoons for those specific requirements. With them, he will discover another versatile quality of the canoe.

Sponsons. Also, canoes may be equipped with sponsons, "built-in"

107

air chambers extending from stem to stern on either side. The added air chambers enhance buoyancy, and are popular with family and summer-camp canoeists concerned with safety while learning advanced skills. Under way, the air chambers do not interfere with paddling ease; only when the canoe is careened will the sponson touch water. Buyers who want a canoe with sponsons must place a special order with the manufacturer for this type of canoe, as these built-in chambers are a part of the original construction of a canoe and cannot be added later.

MISCELLANEOUS ACCESSORIES

Vinyl gunwale covers. These are mainly for aluminum canoes. They snap firmly onto gunwales and provide a flashy line as well as a cushion that eliminates any abrasion of paddles scraped on the gunwale.

Decals identify, decorate, and personalize a canoe. They are available in many permanent, waterproof colors, and are used by most canoe clubs and camps.

Ten-foot setting poles, wood and aluminum, properly piked and ready to use, are available for those who do a lot of canoeing in shallow waters.

A swivel seat with reclining back, mounted to the bow seat of a canoe, adds comfort and efficiency in fishing and hunting situations.

Car-top carrier, with roller, makes it easy to slide a canoe to the top of an automobile.

Many canoe accessories are custom-made by various manufacturers. A catalog with price lists from the firm that built your canoe will inform you of all the accessories available. You have only to ask for it.

Accessories enhance the range of your canoe's value and make possible hunting, fishing, freighting, powering, as well as comfortable cruising, by just plain, relaxed paddling.

PART 3

Canoe-Camping

13

Trip Planning, Tents and Tent Care

Enthusiasts ready to paddle beyond nearby waters find the canoe trip a natural step into adventure. After the first portage—negotiable only with light craft and carefully planned equipment—you leave behind people, traffic, power boats, and the pressures of daily life.

Canoe-camping is like no other recreational trip. Adventurers must pack, stow, and transport all of life's vital components for survival—shelter, clothing, food, first-aid supplies, and canoe-patch kit.

Every one of your needs under way must be anticipated and adequately supplied, for there is no turning back. With proper planning, there is rarely cause for concern about your well-being: with you are all of life's necessities, and independence and self-reliance are sources of rare, deep satisfaction.

TRIP PLANNING

The exacting requirements of canoe-camping dictate its planning: you cannot take along changes of fancy clothes, a favorite lawn chair, cot, or mattress, heavy cans of food, fresh meat and vegetables, cooking grill and charcoal. Obviously, luxury car-camping items are "out."

Long before your trip, amass as much information as possible and

111

acquire your equipment. While poring over maps in the comfort of your living room—a pleasant experience—delineate the trip. Break up your cruise by portaging all of your duffle over land and by changing campsites several times.

Don't let ambition exceed ability, for on location, the picture will be different. Should you schedule an endurance test, it could prove back-breaking and discourage you forever from tripping. Plan for less than you are confident of accomplishing, and your enjoyment will exceed your expectations!

One fundamental principle of success is that all crew members agree on the purpose of the trip; one emphasis—serious fishing, exploring out-of-the-way places, photography, just lazing away the days, or pursuing other special interests.

As a great deal of the time is spent on camping, a little know-how in outdoor skills contributes toward a satisfactory experience and comfort under the stars. Many fine books on camping techniques are available, and each tripper should spend some time at the library to gain insight into outdoor lore.

In preliminary planning, leave nothing to chance. Every crew member should be in on all discussions and debates about each article and piece of equipment. Be prepared for days of rain: if foresight has been exercised, confinement during inclement weather can be enjoyable. Exuberant outdoorsmen, willing to share the work, uncomplaining at the rough spots, and anxious to make the trip a success, are enjoyable tripping companions. Some of the seasoned tripper's most pleasant moments occur when he is tent-bound by rain and high winds for days upon days, reading, writing, and mending gear and clothes in between bull sessions with compatible pals.

SHAKEDOWN CRUISE

A preliminary one-day, overnight, or weekend trip to a local lake or stream is especially recommended for the first-time tripper. Transporting, launching, loading, and operating your canoe under trip conditions will help you gain insights into disposition of cargo, proper trim, and the response of your craft to team paddling. Pitching your tent, unpacking all your gear, and using sleeping bags and cooking utensils will help you gauge the validity of every choice you've made of equipment, clothing, food, etc. Most important, you'll have a basis for revising and polishing your plans for that extended trip.

Should the shakedown cruise be impractical for any reason, at least set out the tent and equipment—unfolded and unpacked—on the back lawn or in a local park, so you can make a complete inspection and check of each item.

TENT

No longer is it advisable to borrow grandpa's heavy wall tent. Tents (like most modern gear) have improved greatly in lightness, strength, and dependability with the use of new fabrics and the improvement of old materials. The design of tents has changed to include outside frames, single inside poles, pop-up, and suspension (from a tree branch) type shelters.

Canvas (waterproof and breathable) still ranks as the ideal tent material. Canvas grades refer to weave, and are judged by weight per square foot, as 8-, 10-, or 12-ounce grades. The 8-ounce duck canvas tent makes a good canoe-camping choice, if closely woven of high-quality cloth and properly waterproofed. Balloon silk and Egyptian cotton are high-grade cotton materials. Nylon and dacron synthetic fibers woven into strong lightweight cloth make ideal tentage. They are also used in combination with cotton, combining the better characteristics of both fibers to good advantage, but are most expensive.

Of the many tent-shape styles, the wall type continues to be popular: it is fairly spacious, with ample headroom. In canoe-camping areas there is no need to carry poles or stakes, because you can hoist the wall tent between two convenient trees, using a rope as a ridge pole, and staking it down. Wall tents come in a wide range of sizes, but the 6½-foot square size with a sidewall two feet high is ideal for the canoe-camper.

The umbrella tent is popular for its roominess, ventilation, sewed-in floor, and water-shedding construction. It is quickly erected by anchoring the four corners with stakes, then lifting the center pole from the inside in a simple, quick operation. A second type is supported by an outer aluminum framework, eliminating the center pole. Bulkiness is its sole disadvantage; the specifically fitted center pole and/or outside frame are integral parts of the structure and cannot be improvised in the woods, hence their bulk must be carried at all times.

The pyramid tent, with its square bottom staked at the four corners and its peak supported by a rope pulled over a tree branch, is the easiest to pitch. The light and compact features, with a floor area measuring 7 by 7 feet, is ideal for fast-traveling campers. This "miner's tent" gives little headroom, and in periods of confinement caused by bad weather it cramps the campers.

The Baker tent, with its awning, open mosquito-netted front slanting to a back wall, gives one the feeling of being constantly outdoors. The entire inside of the tent is open to view, and there is never any groping for articles. The 8-by-10-foot size tent will handily store duffle and adequately protect four campers, especially with a campfire in front of it. This tent, with its open front, though vulnerable to high winds, really enables campers to experience the outdoors, viewing the water-front, watching weather developments, stars at night, sunrise in the morning.

Forester and Explorer tents are ideal for their light weight, insect protection, and water-shedding advantages, but they are, in the main, one- or two-man tents, with little headroom. In the logistics of canoe-camping, tents with greater capacity make better choices by cutting down on the multiple packs. Before everyone goes to sleep, chatter and conversation among four campers is more spirited and morale-building than between two.

Tent Check and Care

Regardless of the tent you choose, these guidelines in camping situations will protect your shelter and add to your well-being.

Does the tent have sturdy, double-stitched seams, and is it reinforced at the peak and the corner pressure points?

Tent rope should be of hemp, sisal, or nylon.

Before a trip, check all lines, frame, or pole parts. Do loose seams or rips need repair? Is a waterproofing treatment necessary? If so, tent makers and sporting goods stores sell waterproofing solutions to spray or paint on tents, duffle bags, tarps, etc. Melted paraffin, dissolved alum, and boiled linseed oil are used by some do-it-yourself campers, but it is more practical to stick to the economical, mass-produced waterproof solutions that are readily available.

In packing and transporting your tent, use a tent bag, or bind it with webbed strapping (rope chafes canvas surfaces).

Getting off the water early gives you time to select a dry site and gather dry wood. Pitch the tent first to protect duffle, sleeping gear, and firewood. Check ground for level area and clear all debris, especially projecting rocks, roots, or snags that may damage the tent bottom.

Should rain threaten in the mid-afternoon, the sensible thing is to stop and pitch your tent immediately. Loosen all lines in the rain, because rope shrinkage may tauten the ropes and pull out the stakes and tent grommets.

Any pressure of the body or equipment against the tent wall during a rain will cause it to leak. Keep all walls free from packs or sleeping gear. When breaking camp, don't pack a wet tent. If you really must break camp in a rain, at the first opportunity, dry the tent to prevent mildew and rotting.

The voyageurs used their canoe as a shelter by turning it over, propping it up at one end, and draping a covering over it. Having to camp at a different site each night led them to perfect this method. (PUBLIC ARCHIVES OF CANADA)

A Tarpaulin or Fly

A tarpaulin or fly arrangement (at least 6 by 6 feet, and preferably larger) on the front of your tent indicates a seasoned tripper. When set up, the tarp's ridge is parallel to that of the tent, and is in reality an extension out front of its roof lines. The tarp can be of light, waterproof tenting, suma, Palina cloth, or a plastic sheet, with a rope ridge down the center and corner and side grommets to which are attached fairly long rope lines. So constructed, it can be pitched in front of the tent with a minimum of poles and effort. Its advantages (in relation to its weight) in both wet and hot weather make it a sensible and valuable addition to your shelter. As floor space is often crowded with

115

sleeping gear, packs, and personal duffle, the tarp offers an extended area of protection. In high winds, the tarp can be set up in a vertical wall position to serve as a windbreak for cooking, camping chores, and warmth.

VOYAGEUR SHELTER

Under certain conditions, when the temperature, wind, and bug concentrations offer no problems, the canoe can be used as a shelter. By turning the canoe over and placing the bedding under it (over a ground cloth and leaf or bough mattress), one sleeper can have a quick shelter for the night. For two, a tarp or poncho can be draped over the inverted canoe and tied down with a rope from the corner grommets to stakes. Also, a long ridgepole, extending the length of the tarp and placed at its center, slanting to the ground, offers a low tent-like shelter.

The canoe, when used as a shelter, should be raised (approximately 12 inches) at one end, propped on a rock or log, and the center thwart may be removed to provide more headroom and comfort. The voyageurs slept this way.

14

~~~~~

Community Equipment

Single indispensable items for the use of all trippers need not be duplicated by each camper.

Repair Kits. Canoe, tool, and sewing kits contain vital items no canoeist should be without when he takes off on an extended trip. The canoe is your vehicle of transportation, your best link with the outside world: therefore, its care and safety must have top priority. Muslin or canvas, ambroid, Duco, or epoxy (or other quick-drying cement) should be carried for the repair of the wood-canvas canoe; a tube of cold aluminum compound for the aluminum canoe; woven-glass cloth, glass mat, and resin adhesive for the fiberglas craft. For temporary repairs in emergencies, waterproof adhesive tape, chewing gum, or spruce or balsam pitch can be used to plug small leaks.

Your tool kit holds materials to put back into service a damaged garment, shoes, motor, packsack, etc., that otherwise would be useless. Pack, in a canvas bag, small quantities of each item, so you have room for greater variety. Here is a suggested list: a small coil of copper or aluminum wire pliable enough to be worked with the fingers, assorted nails and screws, twine, small side-cutting pliers, a small screwdriver, file, and a hone with both a rough and a smooth side. Include air-mattress patches that match the manufacturer's specifications.

The sewing kit should include large- and small-eyed needles, strong nylon or dacron thread, a thimble, buttons, and a small pair of scissors. Also, include a heavy-test, braided fishing line for heavy repairs of your tent and other canvas goods.

First-Aid Kit and Manual. It is hoped that your first-aid kit will be surplus baggage: by being constantly safety-conscious, you should avoid most first-aid treatment. Standard kits are often inadequate in wilderness situations: collect your own. A small-sized tackle box (preferably aluminum) with several compartments is excellent for a larger kit. Line the box with corrugated cardboard or several layers of heavy blotters to prevent breakage. Cover all glass containers individually with sponge rubber or paper tissues held in place by a rubber band. A canvas cover with a carrying strap will enable you to carry the kit over one shoulder.

Include an elastic bandage for support of knees and ankles in sprains and strains, waterproof adhesive tape, a thermometer, tweezers, razor blades, surgical scissors, safety pins, cotton swabs, aspirin or more potent drugs if prescribed by the family doctor, oral antibiotics, cold tablets, alcohol in a plastic bottle, toothache drops, petroleum jelly, antacid, diarrhea and constipation medicines, ointment or lotion for itch and sting from plants and insect bites, sunburn oil or lanolin cream, and specifics your physician recommends for your particular health condition.

An emergency hot water "bottle" can be improvised by wrapping a heated stone or a canteen filled with hot water, in a towel, wool sweater, or flannel shirt.

Keep the *American Red Cross First Aid Textbook* handy for such emergencies as arterial bleeding, stoppage of breath, poisoning, and shock. Master the method of mouth-to-mouth artificial respiration.

Northern canoe country is largely devoid of poisonous snakes, and poses no problem. The canoe-campers in southern, eastern, and some midwestern states should include in their first-aid kits a snake-bite outfit. Don't be overly concerned about poisonous snakes, as they are seldom encountered—and the mortality rate is practically zero. (See Chapter 17.)

Water Purification Techniques. Should there be a question of the purity of the water, make it germ-free: boil it for 10 minutes or add two Halazone tablets to each quart of water and wait 30 minutes. Or add two or three drops of iodine to each quart. In wilderness areas, moving water—whipped by waves, sunlighted, and far from concentrations of men—is often pure and safe to drink without treatment. A bucket dipped from the shore for water often brings up dirt and other material (harmless); therefore, it is better to take the canoe out a small distance and submerge the pail under the surface for clean water. For

118

safety's sake, always inquire locally about sources of safe drinking water.

Insect Repellents. As most trips are made in the summer—at the peak of insect life—effective methods of dealing with mosquitoes, black flies, "no-see-ums," deerflies, etc., are most important for the enjoyment of outdoors. Mosquitoes and other insects rarely fly against the breeze. The location of your campsite is your first step in combating insect irritation. Camp on a high and dry site, exposed to a good breeze.

"Off," "6-12," and "Pellent," easy and pleasant repellents, may be applied to the normal skin, the face, neck, hands, and ankles, as needed. Regardless of your favorite, write in advance for on-the-spot information about local pests and the most effective defense against them. Follow instructions on the can or bottle with regard to the effect on eyes and sun- or eyeglass plastic frames.

Mosquito Netting. Netting is a must on all tent openings. Gaps at the seams and accidental rips may occur in standard tent netting. Take along some Bobbinet material which has a strong, fine mesh that keeps out the tiniest pests. Head nets, purchased or made by campers in advance to use over broad-rimmed hats, are ideal for those with skin sensitivity to repellent liquids. To keep out of the wind, mosquitoes will congregate in the tent, and the camper, ready for bed, will be greeted by them—by the hundreds. A DDT bug bomb is the answer; it is deadly against mosquitoes and most other winged and crawling pests. Before retiring, spray the tent 15 minutes with DDT and malathion in combination in a pressure can with a push-button release. If it is necessary to spray again when campers are inside the tent, breathe through your blanket or pajama sleeve to keep from inhaling the chemicals.

To keep ants and flies from becoming major pests, observe these simple rules: keep all edibles covered; immediately wash soiled dishes, pots, and pans; bury all garbage.

Axe. The axe is the basic wilderness survival tool, and no veteran outdoorsman will venture into the woods without it. The most experienced camper should have the responsibility of cutting firewood, clearing underbrush or overhanging limbs, sharpening tent stakes, and cutting firewood. The ideal tripper's axe is the single-bit Hudson's Bay type, three-quarter size, with a handle length of 28 inches and a weight of about 4 pounds. The axe head should be in a leather sheath when not in use, for the safety of other equipment and campers. At all times, treat the axe with respect, and at night place it in the tent. Don't forget to take along your hone.

Saw. Canoers have come to know the value of a saw for general

119

cutting chores. The saw cuts faster than the axe and is much safer to operate. Collapsible bow saws are light and compact, hinged to fold flat like a sheath over the saw's blade, forming a small package that occupies little space.

Shovel. The army type of folding trench shovel, in which the blade folds back against the handle, has many uses: ditching the tent, digging garbage and latrine holes, removing stones and stumps, putting out a fire, etc. The folded shovel can be readily lashed to a pack for handy carrying.

Candles. Don't underestimate the value of the candle. Use it for sustained heat to ignite damp campfirewood, to furnish heat and illumination inside the tent (protected properly in a tin can or pan!), for friction-proofing the toes and heels of tight shoes, for patching a tent leak, or for sealing leather or canvas seams. With no parts to get out of kilter, no bulbs or batteries or fuel, the candle is a handy foolproof item. Use the thick two-inch-diameter plumber's candle, or household stubs that are no longer decorative.

Inspirator. A piece of rubber tubing (inspirator), small in diameter and about two feet long, is an indispensable device for encouraging a stubborn campfire, especially in wet weather. When one end of the tube is applied to strategic spots at the bottom of the fire and the other end is blown gently, it concentrates the extra air needed to make a smoldering fire burst into flame—very much like the bellows of a blacksmith. Coiled, the inspirator can be conveniently stowed inside a cooking pot. Without the inspirator, you must resort to the old-fashioned method of blowing directly on the fire with your mouth or fanning it with a hat, wildly spreading ashes about.

Waterproofing. Maps, menus, and other vital notes should be waterproofed, as wet paper disintegrates rapidly. If you buy your map from an outfitter, it will be on a good grade of waterproofed paper that stands up well with folding, unfolding, and wetting. Untreated papers can be made waterproof with collodion, clear varnish, or shellac.

Cooking Kit. The popular commercial aluminum cooking kit with nesting pans, coffee pot, lid (which serves as a frying pan), along with plates, cups, and utensils, is an efficient and compact package. Some like to carry it in a sturdy canvas bag with drawstring. Add to the kit plastic salt and pepper shakers, spatula, knife, ladle, can opener, and perhaps a larger frying pan. Aluminum cups, which conduct heat and burn the lips, are best replaced with nesting stainless steel, enamel, or the new nylon cups, which are nick-proof and unbreakable and do not affect taste as did earlier plastic cups. Your dish towels and dish rags help to keep the utensils from rattling. Paper toweling, rust-proof scouring pads, aluminum foil, waterproof matches, and possibly a canvas holder for utensils, round out the cooking-kit needs.

Camp Stoves. Tiny, folding, fuel-burning stoves that weigh a pound or so and fit into the coat pocket, are rapidly becoming a standard item. These small kerosene, bottled gas, and gasoline single-burner stoves give an immediate, intense heat, and burn up to two hours on a half-pint of fuel. Water can be brought to a boil in several minutes, and there are no smoke or ashes to contend with. The two-burner stove folds up like a narrow suitcase, packs well, and if propped against the stern thwart make a solid back rest for a third passenger. In cold, rainy weather, the fuel stove can be set inside the tent or in the doorway for speedily warming the shelter and drying off a damp floor and any damp bedding or clothes. A word of warning: do *not* operate a liquid-burning fuel stove in a closed tent. Always provide adequate ventilation to eliminate the danger of fumes and overheating.

Reflector Oven. On extended trips when it is impossible to carry enough bread, the oven should be considered as a part of the basic cooking kit. A simple but effective contrivance, the oven consists of two square sheets of polished metal, hinged at one end and open at the other, with the baking tray in the middle. The reflector oven, placed in front of an open fire, catches the reflected heat from the angled metal plates and efficiently bakes bread, biscuits, muffins, etc. The metal parts fold flat, and when placed in a bag add little weight or bulk to your load.

Binoculars. A pair of binoculars, carried in the lead canoe, is helpful in scanning the shoreline for lake outlets, landmarks, rapids, suitable campsites, and for observing birds, stars and constellations, and animals.

Camera. A photographic record of your trip can be assured by an experienced photographer who can be designated as the official trip photographer. What constitutes interesting subject matter is relative, and all crew members have their own ideas and may decide to shoot their own masterpieces. Keep your camera where you can snatch it up and use it to record the fleeting glimpses of nature.

Outboard Motor. Many canoeing purists frown upon the increased use of outboard motors in their sport. However, realizing the demand for such power, manufacturers offer square-stern canoe models for the efficient attachment of the outboard. Some canoeists, in order to maintain the many advantages of the double-pointed canoe, use the side motor bracket, or mount, which anchors to the gunwales, extends laterally, and supports the motor at the side of the sternman.

121

Only small, light motors should be used. The 3-horsepower motor is light enough for portage carries, and its fuel economy makes it feasible for some trips. Don't be overly concerned with speed, as fuel consumption is less at slower speeds. European-made motors, light, easy on fuel, with little flash and gadgetry, cruise for more than five hours on a gallon of gas, and you should consider them when buying your canoe outboard.

Log Book. To complement the photographic record of your trip, there should be a written day-by-day account of experiences. One camper can be given the responsibility of recording travel time, campsites, portages, weather conditions, food choices, etc., comments which will provide a good basis for planning subsequent trips. At home, during the cold season, far from clean water, the pictures and log book will brighten the winter reunion in a reliving of the joys of the canoe-camping trip.

15

Personal Gear and Clothing

Each camper carries in his pack some of the community equipment and food and all of his personal duffle. The pack must stow well in the bottom of the canoe and be comfortable on overland carries. The packed tent (rolled or flat), sleeping gear, and cooking kit will probably be set atop the pack, in an efficient carry arrangement.

In various parts of canoeing country, campers seem to have their own ideas of an ideal pack: actually, it boils down to individual preference. An overview of types of packs should help you make a choice.

SELECTION OF PACK

Basically, the packsack is a rectangular canvas bag with shoulder straps, with or without side and inner pockets. These soft packs, with minor differences, are called knapsacks, rucksacks, haversacks, Duluth packs, and several other names. In use, they rest directly on the back of the camper, and their heat-producing characteristic over long hauls is the reason for a minor objection to them.

Alpine Rucksack. To offset the back-hugging pack, many canoeists use an Alpine-frame rucksack favored by mountain climbers and skiers. The framed-type pack includes an enclosed lightweight metal frame arrangement which holds the bag upright and away from the back, allowing air to circulate between the pack and the carrier's back. Several small pockets, stitched to the outside of the pack, make it convenient for storing small and sundry items.

Two sizes of pack racks, and a pack sack with outside back pocket. The pack is tied to a rack. (HIMALAYAN INDUSTRIES)

124

Pack Basket. The pack basket is ideal for the protection of soft, crushable, or fragile items. It is a rigid container, woven of splints of oak or ash, with shoulder straps. The firm pack protects the camper's back from canned goods and other hard objects. The pack basket must be made waterproof by lining it with a plastic bag insert. Its disadvantages are its rigid shape, which prohibits cramming of duffle and foodstuffs, and its inability to be folded for storage when empty.

The Pack Frame. This is an open frame made of tubular aluminum, with a platform on the bottom. Adjustable padded shoulder straps, back-support webbing, and cleats for lashing on a load, complete the simple pack. Duffle bags, sleeping gear, tent—even logs, an outboard motor, cans of water and/or gas, can be strapped to and carried by the pack frame. The *packboard* is similar in principle and utility. The varied duffle loaded on these frames should be protected with a roped-down poncho or tarp covering.

Duffle or Dunnage Bag. The duffle bag used by the military, made of waterproof material and capable of carrying large quantities of gear, serves the canoeist quite well. The duffle bag has no shoulder straps, and must be carried on the top of your pack or by its center handle. The original type with a drawstring on top has been improved by replacing the drawstring opening with a zipper running down one side; thus the entire contents are exposed to view so that you can quickly locate what you need. Duffle bags should not exceed the number of packsacks, because of carrying considerations.

SLEEPING GEAR

A good night's sleep in the outdoors is essential for the health as well as the morale of a group. By following a few simple principles, you will be sure to "sleep like a log."

It is difficult to get experienced campers to agree on which type of outdoor bedding is best, so to eliminate confusion in the welter of available sleeping bags, let's "write off" a few: goose- and eiderdown make ideal fills for sleeping bags intended for sub-freezing temperatures—because of their warmth, light weight, and compressibility—but they are most expensive; kapok fill breaks down with age; wool shrinks; and cotton bags collect and hold moisture.

Ideal for summer use is the sleeping bag filled with a bonded polyester, dacron (fiberfill) 88 that is tough, light, springy, mildew-proof, has great supportive bulk, and fluffs up after being compressed. It is quick-drying. Its compressibility makes it compact when rolled up. Its insulating property is second only to the expensive down materials; and the bulk insulation maintains a uniform thickness of protection under the sleeper's body.

The thickness of a sleeping bag is a good index to its efficiency—the more air and bulk, the warmer the bag. As to shape, the mummy type is restrictive, but occupies less tent space; the rectangular type should have a zipper along one side and across the bottom, and when closed, a draft-free closure at the shoulders as well as around the face.

Recommended for your sleeping bag is a washable inner lining of sheeting or flannel extending the length of the bag, including the head area. Besides making the bag warmer, it can be removed for airing and laundering.

Remember that during sleep, the body gives off much water vapor: therefore, a completely waterproof covering will cause condensation, soaking, and coldness. Only the bottom of the sleeping bag (next to the ground) should be waterproof.

Should your sleeping bag be inadequate for a sudden drop in temperature or for normal early-morning cold, wear a warm sweater or jacket, or add a blanket. A foam rubber mattress gives protection from ground coldness, but it is bulky to pack. The air mattress—make sure it's of rubber-covered nylon with a waffle pattern and a metal valve—is the most used by canoe-campers. It is abrasion-resistant, water-repellent, and mildew-proof. Make sure it is wider than the sleeping bag. Follow this procedure for the proper use of an air mattress: inflate it fully, lie on it, and let out the air until your body contours barely touch the ground, then close the valve. This partial inflation is more comfortable, and you won't roll off the mattress in the middle of the night.

Prepare your bed long before sundown. Check the ground cloth or moisture barrier and the air in the mattress, unzipper the sleeping bag, set down the pillow (if used), and place an extra blanket or sweater and your flashlight at the foot. With these preparations, there will be no need of frantic preparation after the fire has been doused.

CLOTHING

From shoes to headwear, there is little need for specialized clothing if you're oriented to the outdoors with sport or suitable leisure-time apparel. Sturdiness, comfort, and freedom of movement are the main criteria for clothes.

Shoes. The agility required in boarding and beaching a canoe and negotiating the rocky terrain of campsite and portage calls for appropriate footwear. Immediately you can eliminate loose-fitting, unlaced, leather-soled shoes, which become slippery when wet; and ski, hobnailed, cowboy, or high-topped boots are not in keeping with the requirements of canoe-camping.

These young campers use an outboard on their square-end canoe to help transport their duffle and gear to the campsite. Later they will have enough energy left to enjoy their shore activities. (ALUMA CRAFT BOATS)

Basketball shoes, canvas or the preferred leather top, if available, over one or two pair of socks, firmly laced, represent ideal footwear that assures safe footing. Soft shoes are particularly recommended in the wood-canvas and fiberglas canoes, as they do not scuff the floor ribs and planking. Should canvas shoes become soaked, hang them upside down on a line to dry out.

127

Also on your list should be a more sturdy shoe that is warm and supporting, of unlined leather, with an arched inner sole and non-skidding bottom (composition sole). The ankle-high army or G.I. shoe, and the laced moccasin type with rust-proof eyelets, are recommended for extensive hiking. Corfam deck shoes look, feel, breathe, and wear like leather. They stand up under use on rocky terrain, mud, and water, and are easily cleaned with soap and water. The synthetic fabric shoe has been tested and approved by the Council on Footwear of the American Podiatry Association.

Use your shoes before taking them along on a trip: new shoes can be worthless if not broken in properly.

To avoid having wet feet, use a pair of rubbers or thin plastic over-shoes in the dew-damp morning or while hiking in swampy areas. These waterproof overshoes can be slipped on in a jiffy; when not in use, they occupy little space.

Socks. Recommended are wool socks of proper fit, soft, springy, and warm, which can take many launderings. Even when wet, they retain their warmth. Should wool irritate your feet, wear a thin pair of cotton socks under them. Wool socks in combination with cotton, 60-40 or 50-50, if kept dry, are ideal—and cheaper, too.

Trousers and Slacks. Your tripping trousers should meet these standards: proper fit, sturdy reinforced seams, deep roomy pockets, and a button fly. Acceptable fabrics include: sturdy cotton, such as denim, khaki, cotton sateen, water-repellent poplin, and combinations of wool and synthetic fibers. A blend of polyester and cotton is ideal. Launder-ing is one of its advantages: douse in sudsy water, scrub on a rock, rinse in the lake, hang for drip-drying, and in a couple of hours you have trousers that are good and clean, even to the original crease.

The waistband should be large and loose enough to allow you to tuck in thick underwear, a heavy shirt, or a light sweater. A belt at least one inch wide (or suspenders) is important. Veteran Canadian and American outdoorsmen use both. Trousers should be cuffless (iron them out), as turned-up cuffs pick up debris and can cause you to trip while walking over uneven terrain. For protection against rain or wet grass, spray the leg bottoms with water-repellent solution. (This applies also to hats and other clothes that need protection.)

Jeans, frontier style, of heavy denim, cut for women, and/or cotton vat-dyed and sanforized jeans with concealed side zipper, are favorites among women. Ready-made slacks often are too flimsy. For females partial to skirts, an acceptable garment is the wrap-around skirt of high-count cotton poplin, pre-shrunk, and Zelan treated for water repellency. The adjustable wrap-around waistband allows the skirt, with two large patch pockets, to be put on easily. Also recommended is the fan-flared skirt of medium-weight denim, with drawstring waistband. The drawstring fan-folds the skirt for handy packing and carrying. Be wary of impractical trail clothes whose only claim is one of style.

Underwear. To save pack space, take one change of underpants and undershirt: launder as needed. In the clean woods and waters, clothes soil little except from perspiration. Most campers seldom use undershirts, though the Tee shirt is ideal: it can be used as an undershirt, and in hot weather doubles as an outer garment when the shirt is shed. For many reasons, stay away from synthetic fiber underclothes; and don't use the abbreviated, binding type of shorts.

The recently accepted thermal and fishnet underwear materials are ideal: they are comfortable in a great range of temperatures. The hollows in the weave of the cloth trap insulating air and give the body a barrier against coldness—very much as a bird fluffs feathers to trap air and prevent the rapid escape of body heat. The thermal and fishnet undergarments are adaptable enough to be worn under shirts or pajamas, should the weather turn cold. Girls find undershirts of soft material and pants that cover the thighs more comfortable than other styles.

Shirts. Take along only long-sleeved shirts for protection against brush, insects, cold, and sunburn. Shirts should be generously cut to allow freedom of movement, and have two deep breast pockets with button-down flaps. They should have long tails which allow bodily exertion without letting the shirttail pop out. Recommended fabrics include cotton chamois, sturdy-weave army twill, soft pliable synthetics, and fine wool flannel (which is best, but expensive).

Sweater, Windbreaker, or Jacket. The loose, long-sleeved, soft wool sweater is comfortable and versatile. Wear it in camp or while cruising on water when a sudden chill develops and at night when sleeping gear needs support. Use it as a pillow or for shoulder padding when carrying a canoe. The sweatshirts with a drawstring hood and muff pockets are less expensive and are adequate if weather is mild and dry. Also, an all-cotton, heavy-nap, long sleeved, non-sag turtleneck pullover is good. A light windproof, water-repellent windbreaker of tight-woven nylon or dacron over a wool shirt or sweater offers suitable protection from biting winds, without the bulk of a mackinaw. Remember to overlap all breaks in clothing—where shirts join trousers, where pants legs meet socks, etc.

Pajamas. Sleeping apparel should never include clothes you have worn all day. Take along your warmest pair of long-sleeved pajamas rolled in your sleeping bag. Camping nights are generaly colder than expected, and I have discovered the ideal pajamas: heavy fleeced athletic sweatshirt and pants with elastic at the waist and around each ankle, over which I place heavy knee-length wool socks—this is based on the theory that if your feet are warm, you'll be warm all over. Add a bandana or stocking-cap to your noggin, and you will discover these tips to be worth two blankets in warmth-giving advantages.

Headgear. Protection from hot sun and cold weather is a necessity. Light cloth caps with visors are popular and acceptable except in rainy weather. An old crushable felt hat with an adequate brim gives protection from the sun and rain, as does the sailor's cap, which can be turned down to shed rain. The heavyknit navy watch cap has the advantage of folding down over the ears in cold weather. These head-pieces can be folded and stowed in packsacks when not in use.

For the most ideal tripping cap, use the headgear of the voyageurs: the wool beret or tam, which costs very little and lasts a long time. Canadians and Europeans use the beret extensively. It is compact for stowing, offers head protection, will not be blown off, sheds rain, and on cold nights can be worn to bed.

Raingear. Even in rainy weather, there are many chores—securing the canoe and the equipment, supplying adequate wood, preparing food, and checking tent stability—that must be done. To keep from being completely grounded because of rain, you need suitable protection. As your tent and sleeping bag cannot be completely waterproof (or they will be prevented from breathing), so, too, your raingear must give proper ventilation. By locking in all moisture, body-hugging pants and jacket raingear can become steamy with perspiration. Probably the most versatile piece of apparel on a camping trip is the hooded poncho. The earlier stiff army fabric has been improved with the softer, quieter, pliable rubberized nylon material that permits greater move-ment. At the first sign of rain, slip your head through the center open-ing of the rectangular garment with open sides that drape fore and aft. Underway, in a canoe, the poncho protects you from water spray, and can cover duffle. Once ashore, the poncho can serve to cover packs, or as a ground cloth when you're lounging around the campfire.

Ladies, Borrow Male Garments! For the female canoe-camping en-thusiast there are specialized garments. Items that have similar stand-ards for male and female (and can be borrowed without qualm) include: socks, shoes, parka, sweater, jacket, and headgear.

PERSONAL GEAR

Sunglasses. From the earliest times, man has learned to protect his eyes from the reflected light of water, rocks, and snow. For the prevention of temporary blindness and headaches, he contrived a wrap-around shield of bone or bark with narrow slits, and thus was able to pursue his normal activities. Modern sunglasses are not a frill, and should be included in each camper's personal gear. It is to be stressed that the darker the sunglasses, the greater the protection. Skiers use glasses with removable lenses, which is a good idea for canoeists. Amber or yellow lenses are ideal for stormy or overcast weather; like the camera filter, they bring out shadows and improve visual definition. A hard glasses case is a "must" for packing sun- or prescription glasses.

Waterproof Matches. A liberal supply of waterproof wooden kitchen matches should be distributed to all campers (to be carried in their ditty bags) and kept in the cooking kit. The paper-book match is too sensitive to moisture and too feeble to ignite kindling. Dip wooden kitchen matches into melted paraffin or clear fingernail polish. Dry for several minutes, and pack loosely in a plastic tube with a removable lid. Waterproof tubes, as well as wind matches that burn for a minute with an adequate flame, can be purchased from sporting goods stores.

Flashlight. Don't allow the wide range of assorted lamps and gasoline lanterns to entice you from the simple standard D-cell flashlight. A hang-up ring that unfolds from the back end of the case is a useful feature, as is the movable headpiece that can be aimed in various directions (especially good when cleaning fish or washing dishes in the dark). The group may decide on one large boxlike lamp with swiveled spotlight head powered on a single 6-volt battery. The purposeful daytime activity in canoe-camping usually deters nighttime activity: therefore, a minimum of artificial light is required. In stowing your flashlight into the packsack, be careful not to push the button to the "on" position that will light the bulb and wear out the batteries.

Jackknife. The traditional gift to outdoorsmen, a long and thick sheath knife with a curved blade, is not practical for many delicate camp chores and should be left at home—or traded in for a more utilitarian knife. The Boy or Girl Scout knife with its main blade, screwdriver, awl, bottle and can opener, and loop for a lanyard, is an ideal choice for all-round use. A two- or three-blade knife (including one long thin blade for fileting fish and slicing bacon) of high carbon

131

steel, with a grip that fits well in your hand, is also practical. Keep the blades of your knife honed sharp, for sharp knife blades, like sharp axes, are safer.

Life Jackets. It is wise to include a life jacket for each person (swimmer and non-swimmer) in your party, but don't wince: buoyant canoe-wear of today is dressy, lightweight, comfortable, and doesn't interfere with activity. The Empress Jacket (offered by L. L. Bean, Inc.) is lined with millions of air cells, giving both flotation and warmth, like a skin-diver's suit. It comes in various colors and looks like a sport jacket. "Flotherchoc" (import from France), a vest-like, ribbed jacket with belt, worn as conventional apparel, whose air cells give protection from heat and cold plus all the buoyancy you need, is another unobtrusive life jacket.

Ditty Bag. A welter of small stuff, important to each camper, is best centralized in his personal ditty bag. A small version of the duffle bag with drawstring, or the small army type of shoulder bag will serve well. In a sense, the personal ditty bag is a survival kit—for morale and peace of mind. Start loading it with your favorite good-luck charm, then proceed to add: a container of waterproof matches, a small candle, white soap and a towel, clothespins, tooth-brush and powder, folding-type toilet paper, a steel mirror, comb, oil or cream in a plastic container, Chapstick, aspirin, mosquito dope, personal medicine, extra shoelaces, flashlight batteries, bulbs, camera film, razor blades, snippers, a basketball-referee whistle with lanyard, a small coil of fishline, hooks, pencils, a small notebook, paperbacks, large bandana handkerchief, swim suit, Bible, Testament, or Prayer Book, according to faith.

On your person, carry such items as billfold, keys, licenses, permits, compass, matches, folded toilet paper in plastic bag, jackknife, hand-kerchief, and survival ration.

Musical Instruments. Songs and music somehow sound best in the wild. When I hear a favorite piece of music, it is almost always associated—in happy memory—with the river bank, campfire, or the top of a rocky hill overlooking a lake. A good singer in the group, I feel, is as vital as your supply of coffee. Songs in the outdoors can be enhanced and singers encouraged, by the accompaniment of harmon-ica, flute, or Jew's harp—and perhaps, if you're a real troubadour, you might risk taking along a mandolin or guitar.

Fishing Tackle. The canoe-camping trip, paradoxically, works both for and against the serious fisherman: the canoe enables him to reach remote and prolific waters, but because of lack of refrigeration, he can't take out the fish! The "meat fisherman" must tone down his fish-taking ambitions and keep his tackle to a minimum. Baits should be limited to several lures (plugs, spoons, spinners) that adequately cover the range of differing depths—deep water, medium depth, and surface. Rods and reels should be limited to one, even though sneaky campmates add an extra one for insurance against breakage. All rods in the party should be packed in a "store-bought" telescoping case to make an efficient package for stowing in the canoe and carrying over portage trails. Don't forget fishing licenses.

CLOTHING AND GEAR SOURCES

This reasonably complete list of equipment dealers who have adequately served canoeists for many years does not necessarily constitute an endorsement: nor does omission of dealers imply disapproval. It is impossible to cover the scope of acceptable merchandise in the changing developments of modern goods.

Abercrombie & Fitch
  Madison Ave. and 45th St., New York, N.Y. 10017
Alp Sport, Inc.
  2939 Peak Ave. (P.O. Box 1081), Boulder, Colo. 80301
Atlas Sports, Inc.
  800 East St., N.W., Washington, D.C., 20004
L. L. Bean, Inc.
  Freeport, Maine 04032
Bowcraft Sport Shop
  Route 22, Scotch Plains, N.J. 07076
Camp and Trail Outfitters
  112 Chambers St., New York, N.Y. 10007
Canoe Country Outfitters
  629 E. Sheridan St., Ely, Minn. 55731
Don Gleason's Campers' Supply
  Northampton, Mass. 01060
Camp'n Ski (Remington's)
  11230 Georgia Ave., Wheaton, Md. 20906
Gokey Co.
  94 East 4th St., St. Paul, Minn. 55101
H & H Surplus Center
  1104 W. Baltimore St., Baltimore, Md. 21223

Herter's, Inc.
Waseca, Minn. 56093
Highland Outfitters
3593 8th St. (P.O. Box 121), Riverside, Calif. 92502
A. I. Kelty Packs
1807 Victory Blvd. (P.O. Box 3453), Glendale, Calif. 91201
Morsan Tents, Inc.
810 Route 17, Paramus, N.J. 17652
Recreational Equipment, Inc.
523 Pike St., Seattle, Wash. 98122
Robbins Ski Center
323 S. Wacker Drive, Chicago, Ill. 60606
Norm Thompson Outfitter
1805 N.W. Thurman, Portland, Ore. 97209
Trailwise (Ski Hut), Inc.
Box 1, Highlands, N.C. 28741
Woods Bag and Canvas Co.
16 Lake St., Ogdensburg, N.Y. 13669
401 Logan Ave., Toronto, Canada

16

Camp Grub and Cookery

Many a memorable camp meal has been eaten by canoeists in the wilderness. Granted, the fresh air and the exercise whetted their appetites and may have prompted campers to comment on the excellence of the food: but the fact remains that meals whose ingredients have been stowed in the canoe and portaged overland can compete with those served in five-star restaurants.

Careful and detailed thought should go into menu planning and food provisioning. Ample, but not wasteful, appetizing meals of an interesting variety can be enjoyed. The last meal must be carried the duration of the trip: therefore, provisioning the canoe-camping venture must be accurate. In my early years of tripping and guiding, I received cold stares when at the end of a trip there were several pounds of excess food—paddled and piggy-backed for the previous weeks.

Food requirements vary from person to person, and energy-expending activity and bracing weather may increase the need for food. Figure three meals a day and a snack for each person for each day afloat: then add, for good measure, one extra day of food for each. Don't depend on wild berries, fish, or game—they have a way of being scarce when you most depend on them.

Consider your food in terms of both weight that will have to be paddled and the space in the canoe required by bulk. No need to fret about good chow, because nutritious, as well as tasty, meals can be prepared from foods processed by companies which specialize in camp foods. Since water is heavy to transport (nine pounds per gallon), the use of dehydrated, concentrated, and powdered food is mandatory. These foods need only to be restored to their original form by the addition of the missing water, and they are ready to be warmed and served on the trip.

A WORD ABOUT FIRES

Your cooking fire—the hot coals of wood—makes food tastier, as a steak broiled over charcoal and wood chips is much superior to one heat-treated in the city kitchen.

For a fast fire to quick-boil and broil things, use split dry balsam, spruce, white pine, or cedar. For a steady burning fire, use jack pine, chestnut, aspen, or maple. For long-lasting broiling coals, use ash, oak, hickory, or tamarack.

Because menus must take into account individual likes and needs, all members of a group should be involved in their creation. My personal list, in a shirt-pocket notebook printed with India ink and protected with plastic, is merely a suggested eating program. Alter it to suit your group needs. Although seven days are programmed, repeat the meals on a longer trip, or develop your own:

Breakfasts:

1) Apple sauce, mushroom omelet, toast, beverage.
2) Oatmeal with raisins or date flakes, French toast.
3) Stewed fruit, Canadian bacon, biscuits, honey.
4) Orange juice, cold cereal or Cream of Wheat, toast, jam.
5) Prunes, scrambled eggs, hash-browned potatoes.
6) Applesauce, pancakes, sausage.
7) Figs, cornmeal, cheese omelet.

The traditional breakfast beverage is coffee: however, in the instant form, it, tea, and the chocolate drinks fortified with vitamins and minerals (better nutritionally than cocoa) make possible a personal choice.

To make toast, level off the hot coals from the fire, place a slice of bread directly on the coals, and remove it quickly; then turn it over and repeat the process.

The middle of the day is occupied with activity—paddling, portaging, fishing, exploring, improving the campsite, etc.—so a quick, energizing lunch requiring little preparation and no campfire is in order. Also, eliminate the use of cooking utensils.

A camping party on a shakedown cruise tests the newest dehydrated, concentrated, powdered, and freeze-dried foods processed by companies specializing in camping products. (GRUMMAN ALLIED INDUSTRIES)

Lunches:
1) Canned lunch meat or salami, biscuits, honey, mixed nuts.
2) Ry-Krisp, cheese, peanut butter, chocolate bar.
3) Dried fruit, sausage, malted milk tablets.
4) Sandwiches, fig newtons.
5) Dried beef, nuts, raisins.
6) Biscuits, jam, hard candy.
7) Fruit, bacon sandwich, cookies.

Beverages include cold, thirst-quenching drinks made from lemon, orange, and other fruit powders or crystals which include vitamin C and sugar. A pinch of citric acid powder dissolved in cold water is also a real thirst-quencher.

137

To prevent waste, any breakfast leftovers—pancakes, biscuits, oatmeal, etc.—can be used for lunches.

Hard candy is digested rapidly and should be used instead of chocolate if energy-expending activity is on the program.

For the evening meal, I am a firm believer in soup as a first course. A hot bowl of soup on chilly evenings (easily prepared) gives a lift that surpasses the cocktail. Ideal and appetizing are the mixes. They can be fortified with powdered milk and pea or soybean flour, to enhance body. For flavor, add tomato paste, bouillon cubes, onion flakes, pepper, garlic, chili powder, celery or parsley flakes, bacon fat or butter.

Dinners:

1) Broth, canned lunch meat, noodles, vegetable, pudding.
2) Beef bouillon, spaghetti, grated cheese, vegetable.
3) Chicken bouillon, creamed chipped beef, fruit cocktail.
4) Tomato soup, fish, diced potatoes, prunes, lemon.
5) Pea soup, meat course, instant mashed potatoes, pudding.
6) Onion soup, beef stew, biscuits, honey.
7) Vegetable soup, macaroni, diced ham or tinned lunch meat, fruit.

Beverages are the same as for breakfasts. Breads can be pumpernickle, hardtack, pilot bread, large crackers, bannock, or commercial loaves. Because of the air it contains, bread is highly compressible: to facilitate packing, run a kitchen knife through the center of the loaf, and squeeze both ends measurably to reduce its dimension for stowing in your packsack. Should your supply of bread become dry and hard, fry and soften it to a palatable texture (like French toast)—as good as or better than when fresh. Make a batter from powdered milk and eggs, add a little water, and stir. Dip the bread slices, making certain that each side is coated, then fry in bacon fat or butter until soft and golden.

Don't forget the canned butter or margarine for use where needed in the menus.

Macaroni, noodles, spaghetti, and rice provide a wide range of rib-sticking dishes. Add tomato sauce, grated cheese, dried chipped beef, diced lunch meat, bacon squares, corned beef, onion-flavored cream sauce, onion flakes, butter and/or milk to these quick-cooking products, to appetizing advantage.

Hobo style, one-pot meals are tasty and nutritious, and offer variety to the daily menu as well as less labor for the cook.

While in their winter fur-trapping camps, the Cree Indians in Canada keep a huge pot of stew on the fire. As the food is used, they add a rabbit, squirrel, muskrat, bird, or the flesh from their furred quarry, along with vegetables and water, and the pot simmers for days on end with this continuous food supply.

One-pot stews, known as slumgullion, mulligan, and by other local names, are essentially the same in preparation: cut meat into one-inch squares, brown and braise over a hot bed of coals, then place in your large stew pot. Add salt and pepper, and pour in just enough water to keep the meat from sticking. After the meat is browned, add the other ingredients: rice, carrots, onions, white potatoes, peas, diced bacon, and soybean or white flour. Other additions, such as dehydrated soup mix, bouillon cubes, noodles, diced lunch meat, canned peas, etc., can be used. Simmer your creation slowly, but keep the water to a minimum, adding a little from time to time as it boils away. After 20 to 30 minutes of gentle simmering, your outdoor culinary masterpiece is ready.

PROCESSED FOODS

Because of ongoing research in food processing, today camp cookery is a cinch. There's no need to stock pounds of bacon and flour and tins of meat and vegetables, no need to worry about the ingredients of bread, biscuits, pancakes, soups, beverages, etc. Rice, beans, and oatmeal are pre-cooked to reduce cooking time. Potatoes are available in many dry forms (mashed, hash-browned, sliced, au gratin, scalloped). These are but a few examples of the processed wonder foods important to campers.

Bulky foods are out, and as a result of developments in the past few years, weight to be backpacked has been cut practically in half. The variety is wide, and their flavorfulness great.

Several processors offer complete meals, packaged in waterproof bags, that are nutritionally sound and in variety rival the neighborhood supermarket.

These food sources represent all parts of our canoeing country:

Bernard Food Industries, Inc., 1125 Hartrey Ave., P.O. Box 1497, Evanston, Ill. 60204, claim that their "Kamp Pack" cookout food is used all over the world in all types of climate.

Chuck Wagon Foods for Camp and Trail, 176 Oak St., Newton, Mass. 02164, suggest that their non-spoiling foods enable you to amass your grub list in the winter. Besides their self-contained meal packs, the company offers such items as main dishes, cereals, puddings, cake mixes, syrup, and omelets. Emergency survival kits are also offered. As all bags are burnable, there is no problem of disposal of refuse. The meal packs, in waterproof containers, are available for canoeists.

Dri-Lite Foods, 11333 Atlantic Ave., Lynwood, Calif. 90262, tempt the canoe-camper with many meals.

Kisky Foods, 1829 N.E. Alberta St., Portland, Ore. 97211, offer "On the Trail" meal kits containing complete meals, from the main course to seasoning, fat for frying, to the scouring pads necessary for dish washing.

Perma-Pak, 40 East 2430 South, Salt Lake City, Utah 84115, advertise that their dehydrated foods, in cans, will keep for five years or longer under good conditions. The company offers a year's supply of food, bulk grub for large groups, a survival kit that will maintain a person for six days in energy and health; and they ship their products all over the world.

A. D. Seidel and Son, Inc., 2323 Pratt Blvd., Elk Grove Village, Ill. 60007, features a bacon bar—pre-fried, pressed into a bar—that can be crumbled on potatoes and beans, in omelets or flapjack batter. It can also be carried in your pocket and eaten on the trail. The 3-ounce bar is the equivalent of one pound of cooked bacon. Seidel also features, besides a versatile line of daily menus, freeze-dried meats. Their products are packed in plastic bags that will float, and are used extensively in Canada and the United States canoe waters.

One can readily understand that there is little need for wide knowledge of cookery, and that the cooking chores can be passed around to various members of the camping group without jeopardizing the chance of appetizing meals.

Because of modern food processing, the absence of refrigeration on the trail no longer means the exclusion of meat and other foodstuffs that were too long denied the camper. "Dry-freeze processing" are the magic words. The technique, varied and kept secret by some companies, removes moisture under low temperatures, reducing the food in size and making it unspoilable. The structure of the food is not altered, and the addition of water reconstitutes it. This processing has made it possible for soups, meat, potato, and vegetable course meals to be served far from the madding crowd.

Manufacturers who distribute dry-freeze products nationally are:

Borden Co., New York, N.Y.

Campbell Soup Co., Camden, N.J.

Durkee Famous Foods, Cleveland, Ohio

T. R. French Co., Rochester, N.Y.

General Foods, White Plains, N.Y.
General Mills, Minneapolis, Minn.
Golden Grain Macaroni Co., San Leandro, Calif.
Knorr, Best Foods Division, Corn Products Co., New York, N.Y.
Kraft Foods, Chicago, Ill.
Thomas J. Lipton Co., Englewood Cliffs, N.J.
Nestlé Co., Inc., White Plains, N.Y.
Pillsbury Co., Minneapolis, Minn.
Salada Foods, Inc., Woburn, Mass.
Wilson & Co., Chicago, Ill.

For the scientifically minded, in a day of travel the canoeist will use nearly 3,000 calories, which can be obtained from about 2½ pounds of food of high-caloric value.

Older canoe-campers tend to undereat, but bodily needs are met by one's personal reserve of fat—which may be welcome news to some.

Adolescents can easily upset the well-planned rations.

Extended trips tend to increase the food intake of all campers (regardless of age) as they adjust to the wilderness life.

THE VOYAGEURS ATE THAT WAY

I am constantly impressed by the cleanness of the granite terrain of the north canoe country, that rises and falls and then slopes in gradual incline to the water's edge.

The smooth rock surfaces are rain-washed, wind-dried, and sun-splashed. Observing this, I have been prompted, on many occasions, to say, "Dishes are unnecessary, so clean is the rocky table that the bacon and scrambled eggs can be served upon it, and eaten without the least bit of worry about contamination."

Imagine my surprise to find that the voyageurs ate that way! The cook, in preparing the voyageurs' evening meal after a long, hard day of paddling, would use pemmican—an example of early concentrated food—which consisted of dried venison pounded fine, berries in season, and grease. The small bulk, packed into a bag of buffalo skin, had great nutritional value, and being readily available, a handful could be popped into the mouth for quick energy on long, cross-lake, paddling stints. In order to supply a hot evening meal, the cook created a pemmican "Rubbaboo" by adding flour to water, stirring the mixture and bringing it to a boil. Then he would cut off a portion of pemmican mold and place it into the flour-type soup, stirring to blend the grease of pemmican with the milky fluid. The hot gruel was ladled into voyageurs' dishes, but since it was too hot to eat, and the voyageurs were too hungry to wait, they poured the "Rubbaboo" into small hollows of rocks where it cooled rapidly and was immediately eaten with gusto.

17

Cruising Considerations

In preparation for your trip, you study maps, books, and pamphlets, correspond with outfitters and suppliers, consult with seasoned canoeists, test specially processed foods, and go on at least one shakedown cruise. You carry, launch, and—observing the principles of balance and buoyancy—you load your gear and duffle at your starting point.

Wait, before you board your canoe! Have you given your route and approximate timetable to your parents, friends, outfitter, and/or the local official: ranger, park officer, game warden, or Mountie?

All travelers in the wilderness areas of Canada are required to file. At first, the need of a detailed declaration, to park officials, of our intended adventure bothered me. I reasoned that when Canadians enter the States no one asks them, "Do you intend to travel west of the Mississippi River, south of the Mason-Dixon Line, or points east?" Then the logic became clear: the safety of all canoeists is of concern to Canadian officials. When they know where you plan to be and at what time, they can dispatch emergency crews to bring you out of danger zones should a violent storm, forest fire, or flood occur.

Your trip plan filed, board your canoe and check the trim. The bow should be slightly higher than the stern; to insure safety the freeboard (after the crew is aboard) should be not less than seven inches for smooth water, and more for large lakes. With proper trim you will discover the reassuring stability and response of your canoe, and you will be able to ride heavy seas with little risk.

In a two-canoe party, to assure self-contained units, the food, cooking utensils, tents, and tools should be divided as equally as possible between the two. Don't forget an extra paddle in each canoe! While wilderness canoeing in Canada, each 18-foot freighter canoe carried four passengers with complete outfits: four sleeping bags in a waterproof duffle bag, tent, cooking kit, axe, packsacks with personal duffle, and food. Thus each canoe was a self-sufficient unit, with all essentials independently transported.

When two or more canoes are used, the more experienced canoeists occupy the lead canoe. The others should stay close behind. It is advisable to keep up a constant chatter and banter between canoes, discussing map course, sights along the way, hazards, developing weather conditions, portages, and possible campsites.

At all times while under way, each crew member keeps his whistle, compass, and waterproofed map on his person, and his raingear and camera (should he choose to bring one) within reach. All members share the responsibility of the cruising route, "two minds being better than one," especially when seeking tricky outlets from a lake, avoiding going up dead-end fingers of water, and—in large lakes—following proper direction around the many islands. The identity of land masses—peninsulas, islands, and mainland—offers challenges that generate many opinions, and decisions about the proper route are best made by all in the party.

YOUR COMPASS IS ALWAYS RIGHT

When returning to familiar waters after a drought, I have discovered that many different land contours at the water's edge tend to refute earlier observations. In high water, points and peninsulas were submerged, to give an entirely different configuration to the shorelines.

Although the validity of the compass often is suspect, it is always right! Your sense of direction is not instinctively great, as some outdoorsmen believe. A number of experiments indicate that man, in the absence of familiar landmarks, will travel in a complete circle, left or right. All crew members should refer constantly to their instruments of travel (compass and map), and when a question arises, check out each other's opinions.

Most wilderness canoe waters are located in the northern part of the hemisphere, where the declination of the compass needle must be understood. The geographic North Pole represents the true north, while the compass needle points to the north magnetic pole, which, in varying degree, points to a section of far northern Canada (north of Hudson Bay). The two poles are not identical. The closer to the North Pole a canoeist navigates, the greater the compass error of true north. Most maps include a diagram indicating the amount of declination for the region it covers. For true orientation, the canoeist must take into account the degree of correction needed between the compass needle pointing to the north magnetic pole and the geographic North Pole.

SOME TIPS TO USE WHILE UNDER WAY

While cruising along, whether on a rock-strewn river or an open lake with strong wind and high waves, the bowman is the tactical commander of the crew: it is his responsibility to keep the craft on a safe course. The bowman's knowledge of paddle strokes should enable him, as conditions warrant, to brake the canoe, to turn it sharply left or right, or to continue straight ahead. Little wonder the bowman was paid more than the stern paddler during the fur-freighter day of the voyageurs.

Plot your cruising route to take advantage of shelter from the wind furnished by islands and shores with high bluffs and trees. Safety considerations dictate the choice of a longer course rather than the most direct when taking into account such windbreaks.

Should a strong wind develop, never allow the waves to hit your canoe broadsides. Should your direction be into the wind, turn the bow for "quartering" (slicing the waves at an angle of 45 degrees or less). The wind, slanting off your course, will, in effect, move the canoe in a tacking maneuver. Instead of a direct course, it will be necessary to follow a series of zigzag legs to reach your destination. Paddle steadily for control of the canoe; don't permit the wind to dictate its course or its speed.

Should your canoe begin to ship water from waves, get off the seats. Paddle from a kneeling position on the bottom of the canoe, leaning against the seat, with your knees well apart for better bracing. This will lower the center of gravity of the canoe and add to its stability.

The seasoned tripper prepares for rough water and keeps his cargo high and dry by raising it a few inches from the floor; he stows it on

145

a bed of evergreen boughs or on a packboard. In addition to soaking duffle, shipped water affects the control of a canoe. As soon as possible, bail or sponge it out.

Also, the sternman moves slightly forward to raise the stern. Should the heavy sea increase in velocity, and/or rocks peril your way, im-

Hunter-fishermen in an aluminum canoe designed especially for trips to remote spots. The sturdy, heat-treated aluminum withstands the rigors of running rapids, yet is light enough to make portaging easy. The 17-foot canoe weighs 78 pounds but has a capacity of 800 pounds. Note that the men are paddling in a kneeling position, that the stern-man has moved forward, and that the bow is heavy for better control while traveling up rapids. (MIRRO ALUMINUM CO.)

provise an anchor: tie a bucket to a 10-foot line (firmly attached to the stern), and trail it behind. Do not tie it to the stern top deck, as the anchor will tend to pull down the stern. The attachment should be made to a bridle—a loop of rope through the stern seat, down both sides of the canoe and tied at the keel, where the anchor rope is attached.

If you cannot make it to shore to "hole up" for the duration, and the wind upsets the canoe, remember one simple, important rule:

STAY WITH THE CANOE!

Whether upside down or right side up and filled with water, the

146

canoe will remain afloat. Stay with it: hold onto the upturned keel amidships (if overturned), or onto the gunwale, deck, or lines. Rescue as much floating gear as possible, but do not swim too far away from the canoe. While you hold onto the canoe, the wind eventually will take you and the craft to shore. You can help things along by using a flutter or frog kick to push the canoe. There's no hurry, so take your time and take frequent rests. Figure things out and keep your cool.

Upsetting a canoe is rare, and usually is the result of showing off, of carelessness, and of disregard for the principles involved in proper balance when loading a canoe or when cruising. During thousands of miles of cruising in the States, Canada, Guatemala, and Europe, the author has never fallen into "the blue." Should an accident occur, there is little danger to your safety if you STAY WITH THE CANOE. Many Indians who spend their lifetimes in canoes, carrying families of 10 children, a half-ton of moose meat, and hunting and fishing, without ever upsetting, do not know how to swim.

PORTAGES

Anticipate turbulent stretches of water in river travel from careful study of the elevations and symbols within your location on your map. A considerable difference in elevation of land from one point to another within a short distance indicates a drop of water level in the form of falls or rapids: therefore, it is necessary for the bowman to be alert for these drops and give the proper signal in ample time to portage.

Land declivity adds to the interest of a canoe trip. On level stretches, the smooth, unseen power of water has its appeal, but the lacy foam of falling water and the swirl of rapids bring an interesting change to the river's mood. The power of the water rouses the eyes and the ears as it tumbles and roars, then at the new-found level, it reorganizes and moves quietly on its way.

Only the expert canoeist should attempt to shoot the rapids—and very few do. They neither imperil their personal safety nor that of the craft and equipment by foolhardy risks. In fact, early fur traders in the employ of the Hudson's Bay Company were forbidden to endanger man and craft by shooting rapids.

Be especially vigilant about the fatigue factor. Late in the day, when the canoeist is anxious to make time and feels too tired to carry packsacks and the canoe, he is apt to take more risks. Guard against the

147

temptation to save time and energy.

In approaching a portage, it is of great importance to determine the proper takeout side, for there you will find the easiest, shortest, blazed trail. Used for thousands of years by the Indians who came to the region after the Ice Age, these trails predate the voyageurs. The Cree Indians of northern Ontario place a pole on the shore to indicate the takeout side. Often the portage trail is hidden by weeds and undergrowth, so that you have to make a thorough search for it. Even though the path weaves, rises, or falls, it is always the most advantageous to follow—neither do the Indians wish to work unnecessarily.

In portaging, it is best to unload (or load) a canoe while it is waterborne and parallel to the shore (alongside docking). If necessary, one crew member wades alongside the canoe and transfers the duffle to crewmen on shore. First the canoe is carried across the portage. Break up long portages by carrying duffle in quarter-mile (more or less) relays. Drop the load and return for another, bringing it forward in a second stage. In this way, you combine labor with a return, recuperative hike. Also, you might deter a porcupine or raccoon from chewing your paddle and packsacks. You are in good company when you take a portage with sensible rest stops. The voyageurs, when toiling over a long portage, set down their loads at a designated place—known as a *pose*—then went back for the next load.

In many canoe-camping areas, every half mile or so there are rest stops where canoes can be leaned on crossbars. After your rest, you can shoulder the canoe without having to raise it from the ground. On trails lacking these canoe supports, use the crotch of a tree, or rest your craft between two trees growing close together.

One summer, on a canoe trip to Superior-Quetico, we had finished our portage of Wheel Barrow Falls, and while resting on the shore, watched the use of a new (to us) technique of lifting a canoe to the shoulders. A fine college-age lad stood alongside his canoe, knee-deep in water, near the shore. He heaved the duffle to his partner on the bank, then flipped the canoe, which was riding waist high, onto his shoulders. He sloshed ashore and followed the trail with no lost time. The position of the canoe—floating high—made only a short lift necessary, and he easily managed to shoulder it. This technique might be used when racing against time: however, walking a considerable distance in wet shoes is an invitation to foot trouble.

Northern canoe trails are practically devoid of harmful snakes. However, in central and southern regions, where they live (which can be ascertained from natives), take these precautions: (1) include a snake-

148

bite kit in your first-aid materials; and (2) take extreme care on paths, especially when climbing bluffs and cliffs. The snake is dangerous when approached suddenly and startled. Make a lot of noise, and while climbing or descending hills, toss rocks ahead on the path to send any sun-bathing "critter" scurrying from your path.

In shallow streams, it is expedient for the bowman to get out and, while wading, pull the canoe through shallow water, around boulders and other obstructions.

TRACKING A CANOE

In certain portaging situations, where the path may be difficult, while the shoreline of the rapids is free of overhang and ledges and provides good footing, a method of hand towing (tracking) may be used to good advantage. Tie a 50-foot line to the bow thwart and another to the stern thwart. With a firm grip on the lines, start walking upstream along the bank, towing the canoe. Releasing the bow line while pulling the stern line will drive the canoe farther out into the stream. Pulling the bow line while releasing the stern line will bring the canoe closer to your side of the water. Walk slowly, and constantly watch the reaction of the canoe. One man can be in the canoe helping with paddle or pole to steer the craft around boulders and obstructions. Take extreme care, however, for a quick jerk by the man with the lines may upset the passenger in the canoe.

If the water velocity is not great, another method of tracking is the use of a single line tied to the bow. As the puller walks along the bank, his companion keeps the craft off shore with the aid of a long pole. Watch the effect of the current for snags and the reaction of the canoe. Check and doublecheck the knot on the rope, and make certain that the line is strong, as the current places great strain on the rope. My first experience with tracking in a remote wilderness area resulted in a breakaway because of weak rope. The canoe went bobbing crazily down a series of rapids, shipping water, before coming into a quiet eddy where it was retrieved. There was no loss beyond wet duffle—beginners' luck!

By beginners, portages are looked upon as hard work. They claim that there are two types of language on a canoe trip: one is the talk around the campfire; the other is reserved for portage trails. And once I asked a returning canoeist if the next portage was an easy one. "There are no easy portages!" he replied.

I find portages an interesting change of pace in the outdoor program, especially on long cruises. The hike gives one the opportunity to stretch and use different muscles. The walleyes and small mouth bass feed in the pools below water turbulence. Many times we have caught fish there, cleaned them on the smooth rocks, and packed the filets for the evening meal.

CRUISING SAFETY

Always be alert to danger signals—whether they be water, weather, wind conditions, or horseplay on the part of your paddlemate. A person who uses bad judgment in the wilderness is not only a pest, but also a danger. Remember, the canoe is dangerous only if used improperly. There is basically no difference between safe canoeing, sky-diving, surfing, skiing, automobile racing, or scuba diving, where a little hazard exists, but proper training and respect for the rules of these recreations are the basis of pleasant experiences.

Man is not an aquatic being. He must learn to swim, to develop confidence while in the water, and to respect its danger and power at all times. Waters in the vicinity of 60-degree temperature can produce a dangerous chill with hazardous effect. Loss of consciousness is possible after an hour in such water, and no matter how good a swimmer thinks he is, his skill is useless if he's unconscious in the water: thus the life preserver which keeps the face out of water has a definite survival value.

The canoeist should be able to swim, to float, to tread water, and to swim under water. At all times when in a canoe, non-swimmers should wear a life jacket. One qualified swimmer should accompany each non-swimmer. Always take a buddy in a canoe; never go out alone. Take advantage of instruction in water safety from The American Canoe Association, 400 Eastern St., New Haven, Connecticut; The American White Water Affiliation, 1925 Hopkins St., Berkeley, California; your local chapter of the American Red Cross, and the Y's, Scout groups, or local parks.

You won't need a great deal of swimming skill if you obey the simple rules: never stand in a canoe, keep weight low and centered in the canoe, refrain from sudden and abrupt movements, and never leave a capsized canoe.

In cruising situations, when the canoe is fully loaded, do not cast or troll for fish. Your troubles will begin if you hook a really big one. In the evening, after dinner, is the time to do your fishing. Cast from rocky shores, where the footing is good for a wide casting range. Should you fish from a canoe and latch onto a big one, remember the principles of canoe balance: do not lean over to play the fish— allow the rod to do the work as you keep to the center line of the craft balance. Don't force in the fish; make it fight the rod, and eventually your prize will be subdued and tame enough to bring in.

When you are paddling along, if the day gets hot and calls for a refreshing swim, take the canoe to a sandy beach, pull it ashore, then go for your dip. No matter how good a swimmer you are, never dive from a canoe in mid-lake. The wind can blow away an empty canoe, riding high in the water, so that even an Olympic swimmer could not catch up with it.

WEATHER AND SAFETY

It is important for wilderness travelers to be weather conscious and to possess some weather savvy, for weather is a constantly changing phenomenon. The sun is the prime force that affects weather. Its rays heat the water, the earth, and the air, in uneven intensity, to cause winds, clouds, thunder, and rain. Weather creates its own signs in the form of clouds, fog, heat or cold, humidity, and wind. These signs are observable or can be sensed: learn to read them, keeping in mind that positive predictions, even for meteorologists with instrumentation, are dependent upon many changing factors that defy accurate prediction.

Be prepared at all times for changes in the weather. Get into the habit of constantly watching the sky for cloud formations, density, and build-up. Be alert for wind changes, drops in temperature, and humidity. Weather adages (some dating back to 400 B.C.) are helpful, for many are based on scientific facts.

Include a few weather maxims in a small notebook and carry it in your shirt pocket. You will find that you can forecast changes in the weather with a degree of accuracy and eliminate many risks in wilderness travel. "Red at night, sailor's delight," and "Red in the morning, sailor's warning," have withstood the test of time, as has "Heavy dew in the morning indicates good weather; no dew means rain." Also, "A rainbow in the morning means bad weather: a rainbow in the evening indicates good weather." Smoke from a campfire can be a weather indicator: when it rises in a long, thin spiral, good weather is ahead; when it is sluggish and rises only a short distance, drifts away, and then settles, a change—probably rain—is on the way. Clouds moving in different directions, on two different levels, the lower stratum racing under an overcast sky, indicate unpleasant weather ahead. When the moon is white, clear, and bright, plan to travel in the morning. When a halo or ring surrounds the moon, or when the moon is red, look out for rain.

We cannot control the weather, but we can anticipate its capricious behavior and prepare to cope with it for our comfort and safety.

It is difficult to prepare the canoeist for all the situations, good and bad, that may arise on an extended canoe trip. Every canoe trip is different; every trip is unique! Therefore, it is impossible to predict its unfolding, because it is impossible to prepare for every exigency. Each trip requires adjustment to unpredictable situations and hence becomes a learning experience. Every veteran canoeist, regardless of the water miles behind him, knows that the present trip will be different, unique—and that's the adventure of canoe-camping; to go boldly forth, with all of life's necessities, with no concern for the morrow, with confidence in his craft, with personal skill and judgment.

With their canoe unloaded and camp pitched, these travelers have leisure time for fishing in Nogies Creek near Peterborough, Ontario, a part of the Kawartha Lakes chain. The deep, still water is well stocked with small-mouth bass, pickerel, and pan fish. (CANADIAN GOVERNMENT TRAVEL BUREAU)

18

$\sim\sim\sim\sim$

Life at the Campsite

In tripping adventures, most of the time is spent camping: therefore, it is necessary to bone up on outdoor-living techniques. It is also essential to have the right companions—dependable, compatible, with common sense—who enjoy all the aspects of a trip: paddling, pitching camps, cooking, washing dishes, and clean-up chores.

PITCHING YOUR CAMP

Begin to look for a campsite well before sunset. On the first day out much motion is wasted, so allow about three hours of daylight to set up camp. In subsequent pitching (as teamwork develops and less time is needed), one hour will be ample time in which to cook, eat, wash dishes, and make everything shipshape in time for an evening of fishing and a campfire session.

Your camp location selected, bring the canoe ashore by beaching or alongside docking, unload gear, then carry the canoe safely from the water and turn it upside down away from the water's edge.

On regular canoe trails, often your campsite will have been established by former campers, and ditching trenches previously used can serve your tent. If you are the first in an area, there are certain points to consider. Though it is impossible to find a campsite with a combination of good features, look for one embodying as many as possible: an elevated clearing with porous soil, a beautiful view, privacy, a certain amount of isolation, an open spot just on the edge of a stand of trees, and a level area with good ventilation. A breezy elevation is a deterrent to mosquitos but offers a fire danger: therefore, your fire bed must be depressed or banked with logs or rocks on the windward side.

Some things to avoid: pitching a tent under tall trees that will drip for hours after a rain; lush, tall grass that indicates water-soaked ground; low areas that can become inundated in a sudden rainstorm; rotten trees infested with ants and other insects; sandy beaches whose fine grains permeate clothing, food, and gear. Don't be tempted to pitch your tent over mossy surfaces. In the north, pillows of quilt-like moss add a softness to hard granite and are beautiful to behold, but without a root system, the moss absorbs nutrients and moisture from the air and becomes a sponge that squishes and oozes when you sit or lie on it.

The numerous chores involved in pitching camp require the help of all hands and result in beehive activity. This is no time for fishing, sightseeing, or pursuing personal projects. First, clear the tent site and set up the tent. If possible, face the tent opening north or northeast in an area that will receive the morning sun to evaporate the morning dew and to get you up early. The tent erected, lay down the ground cloths and sleeping gear and store your personal duffle.

Kitchen and Wood Supply. Decide upon a kitchen area for your cooking fire and for stacking firewood; place all cookery and eating equipment in position. Should there be no prior fire location, scrape away all inflammable material from a spot five feet in diameter, and keep the fire away from trees, logs, or brush.

In gathering firewood, select dead trees (never chop a live one), stack them near the fire, and cover them with a tarp or bark slabs. The firewood-chopping detail should be assigned only to an experienced tripper who knows about safe axemanship: clothes that allow freedom of movement, a secure stance, adequate clearance on backswing and overhead, smooth and easy stroking, and carrying the unsheathed axe by grasping the grip on the handle close to the axehead. When splitting wood, never place your foot on the log to be cut, and never cut wood on the ground. Use a chopping block, a low stump, or a section of a log, for small stuff like kindling, tent stakes, etc. For larger pieces of firewood, place a heavy log on the ground and use it as a chopping block. The wood to be split is placed on the far side of the chopping block (away from the chopper), at right angles; you strike where it contacts the chopping log. If hit in the middle, the split wood will spring up in dangerous flight. Proper axemanship can be learned from a good teacher and lots of practice; proficiency cannot be taught by narration. Proper respect for the axe is extremely important, as it probably represents the most dangerous piece of equipment in camp. Great caution in the use of the axe is always necessary. Remember to keep your axe out of reach of the weather; at night lay it sheathed and flat in the tent to protect it from dampness and handle-chewing porcupines.

The cooking fire should be built early enough so that it has burned down to coals by the time the cook is ready. The first meal should include perishable foods, and, because of the busy first-day schedule, should be one that is easily and quickly prepared.

Before dinner, should a refreshing, cleansing dip be decided upon, wade out to your swimming hole to ascertain depth, the presence of boulders, sharp rocks, sand bottom, etc. Never dive into strange waters.

CLEAN-UP AND SANITATION

While eating dinner, place on the fire a large pot of water for dish-washing. This procedure consists of scraping plates, washing them in hot soapy water, rinsing them in hot water, and drying them over heat or in the sun, then packing and storing them away from flies. After evening meals, scald dishcloths and towels and hang them out to dry.

Garbage Pit. If your campsite doesn't have a disposal pit, burn and bury your garbage. Solid wastes that will not burn, such as aluminum foil, fruit peelings, etc., should be buried. Tin cans, especially, should be burned to soften the solder so that you can mash them to a minimum thickness with your heel. Burning causes tin cans to rust and decompose quickly in the ground in a minimum of space. Crumble paper and tend it with a green wood poker. Check burning paper and light inflammable material that flies in the air and could produce a fire hazard.

Grease Pit. Liquid wastes, such as dishwater and waste fats, should be poured into a grease pit—a hole in the ground downslope from camp, lined with stones or gravel to act as a filter. Burn out the grease pit periodically with a quick-burning fire, using kindling, leaves, or paper.

Latrine. Most well-used canoe campsites have latrines, but should you need to make one, the straddle trench or pit is easy to dig. Dig

155

the latrine a hundred feet or so away from camp and water supply. Pile the dirt from the two- to three-foot deep trench along its side, from where it can be kicked or shoveled back into the trench each time after use. Should you decide to stay at one campsite for several days, purify the latrine periodically with wood ashes or chloride of lime, which can be purchased at a lumberyard. Buy several pounds and pack it in a waterproof bag. Also, erect a sitting support. Use one log or two (set parallel) about 18 inches above the ground for a comfortable seat above the pit. Place the latrine in cover to insure privacy, which can be increased with the addition of a canvas or tarp wall.

Once, when our family went uranium prospecting in the mountains of Utah, we enjoyed a fancy outdoor latrine. I found a discarded buckboard seat, sawed away the center panel, and placed it between two huge branches of a recently fallen cottonwood tree. The foliage, still intact, provided privacy, and the ornate curved iron side rests lent a flair of luxury.

BEDDING DOWN FOR THE NIGHT

In camp, going to bed is not simply a matter of adding extra night clothes for a chilly night and hitting the sack. There are responsibilities in camp security, equipment protection, and personal preparation that must be met each night.

1) Check to see that the canoe is well out of the water and secure, so that a night wind cannot blow it into the water.

2) Cover equipment that is not waterproof. Securely hide from gnawing animals such items as candles and soap. In danger also are the perspiration-soaked axe and paddle handles which are good sources of salt for porcupines. Note: some campers place loose pots and pans on their upturned canoe that shelters equipment; when it is disturbed, the rattle of metal will act as a backwoods burglar alarm.

3) Provide ample water and wood supply for quick preparation of breakfast.

4) Extinguish fire completely, as a high wind can fan smoldering ashes into a flame.

5) Spray inside of tent with a bug bomb.

6) Before entering your sleeping bag, safeguard your glasses (if worn) by placing them in a hard case or inside your shoes for safekeeping. Place your shoes and flashlight beside your sleeping bag where you can locate them quickly in the dark.

7) By popular and unanimous demand, the retiring hour will be ignored if Mother Nature decides to present her north woods' spectacular. The Northern Lights are a breath-taking phenomenon that have, on many occasions, kept us spellbound till the wee hours, so majestic were the patterns of moving light across the heavens: shafts of magenta, curtains of purple, broad serrated arches of polar white—the mysterious lights constantly moving in changing configuration on the biggest stage in the world!

You and your pals lie on your backs, on a high and smooth boulder, comforted by the heat-retaining qualities of granite after a day's sun. The spectacle is not limited to the north—the patterns of stroboscopic light cover the zenith down to the horizon in all directions—north, east, south, and west. If I were to name things that best typify the vastness and grandeur of the north, they would include the silent sky spectacular of the Northern Lights, and the plaintive, quavering wail of the loon.

CAMP SCHEDULE

A certain amount of organization—personal and group—is necessary in a camping situation. For the well-being of all, follow a flexible schedule of getting up, preparing and eating meals, doing camp chores, fishing, sightseeing, and/or engaging in your special-interest activity.

As in your daily home life, rules of health and standards of grooming should be followed: daily baths, clean underwear to prevent chafing and infection, clean socks to prevent blisters, and, of course, brushing teeth, shaving, and combing hair.

In regard to group well-being, do your share in keeping the camp in order, safeguarding and respecting equipment, supplying wood and water, washing dishes, disposing of garbage, and helping to develop a pleasant group spirit.

All activities in your new setting should be in low key, in a tempo that fits the environment. Nature is unhurried, why should you not be? Don't complain about the rain—it will stop. If the fish don't bite—there's another day. If the cook burns the food—take over the next time.

KNOW YOUR WOODED NEIGHBORHOOD

It is good trip planning to lay over at the first campsite for a few days to adjust to the different way of life, the new environment, your schedule, etc. In a group conference, precisely locate your camp on the map, and note the distances and time of travel to fishing areas, scenic points, and especially to your base outfitter and automobile.

At the first opportunity, with compass in hand, explore your newly adopted neighborhood. Wearing heavy shoes, hike in a group to discover the nature of the land. Scale the highest point and look around. Note all possible canoe-docking areas, so that in the event of unfavorable wind which prevents your use of your chosen docking site, you have an alternate in mind. Should you be on an island, explore its boundaries.

Your whistle (like your compass) always should be on your person. In times of distress, use the universal signal of three blasts. All outdoorsmen and sailors use that signal: three shots from a gun, three bonfires, three flares or rockets, etc. Never use three for any other reason. If temporarily lost, don't panic and wander aimlessly about. *Sit where you can be seen.*

Other canoe-campers, sharing your interests, are congenial people, and most enjoy company. Visit them (with biscuits and jam) and exchange accounts of experiences: fish battles won and lost, animals observed, favorite recipes, camping techniques, etc. You will learn from them, and they (you hope) from you, of prolific fishing spots, ideal campsites, portage trail conditions, and other vital information.

BREAKING CAMP

When you have broken camp, the area of nature's kingdom that you have used should show little evidence of your tenure. It should be helped to return quickly to its natural state of beauty, which will be possible only if every bit of litter has been burned or buried. Make certain that you cover latrine, garbage, and grease pits. Sticks placed upright above them indicate your consideration for the next campers.

Be sure to extinguish completely your fire. On one trip I made to northern Canada (Pikangikum), with Dr. Harold Emiley and Dr. Robert Kuehnert, we lost an empty duffle bag by leaving it near a supposedly extinguished fire. While we were involved in lake and shore activities—swimming, fishing, washing clothes—a gust of wind fanned sparks and blew them onto the bag. Although no fire resulted, the bag smoldered and was completely destroyed. The thick carpet of humus in the deep forest can conceal smoldering embers that remain under the soft overburden, and later a strong wind can whip them into flame. Douse your fire thoroughly with a pail of water; wait a few minutes, scratch the surface with a stick, then douse again!

Cache some firewood in a sheltered, rainproof area. The next camp group may arrive late, during a rain, or too tired to scrounge for wood for that first meal and warmth. You can feel no greater pride in fellow-campers than when you find a supply of wood upon arriving at a campsite. The multiple tasks of camp erection are eased. Respect the unwritten Law of the North obligating the camper to leave at a campsite at least as much firewood as he found on arriving.

Before bidding adieu to your campsite, in your notebook write a running account of such items as logistics of the trip, paddling times, campsite, portages, map reading, landmarks, all of which can serve as guidelines for your next trip. Refinements in lists of food, clothing, equipment, and sleeping gear will help you the second time around.

PART 4

Adventure on Wide Horizons

19

Modern Voyageurs: Competitions, Activities, and Organizations

Spectacular feats were added, in 1967, to the long history of the canoe, during which brave men used the craft to engage in seemingly impossible exploits: Francis Brenton, alone, crossed the Atlantic Ocean in a specially rigged canoe; and the Canadian Expo '67 Voyageur Race, requiring 104 days (from May 24 to September 4), covered 3,283 miles.

FRANCIS BRENTON

"Tough Adventurer Starts Lonely Voyage from Chicago to Africa," "Across the Atlantic by Canoe?," "Brenton's Saga Ended by Crew of Russ Tanker," "Sails Ocean in Solo Canoe"—newspaper headlines proclaimed as all America saluted a feat that was consistent with earlier valor, when strong men sailed in wooden ships.

The 5-foot-10 adventurer, weighing 150 pounds, self-admittedly accustomed to hard manual labor, possessing a tough hide, sound stomach, and an ability to push his body beyond comfortable limits, was at thirty-nine a seasoned sailor. He was born in Liverpool, England, and after soldiering for the British Army in Korea, Malaya, and India, he made the world his beat. His book, *Long Sail to Haiti,* describes his 1962 solo sailboat voyage from the Canary Islands to Haiti. In 1966,

163

Brenton canoed from Cartagena, Colombia, to Chicago, weathering Hurricane Alma.

The logistics of the trip represent the quintessence of planning—of import to all canoeists, regardless of the type of trip they schedule.

Francis Brenton making a final check of the *Sierra Sagrada* (*Holy Mackerel*) in Diversey Harbor, Chicago, before leaving on his one-man canoe trip to Africa by way of the Great Lakes and the St. Lawrence Seaway, then across the Atlantic. (CHICAGO TRIBUNE)

Once committed to the sea, Brenton discovered that his plans, well laid ashore, were difficult to follow—the lament of many canoeists during long trips.

The Sierra Sagrada (Holy Mackerel), Brenton's canoe craft, was in reality a catamaran with a decked-over San Blas Indian fishing canoe, 26 feet long. The second hull was a triangular pontoon 20 feet long, the bottom point edged downward, giving the topside a deck surface similar to that of the canoe. Four-by-four wood timbers held together the two hulls, while two masts supported main, mizzen, and jib sails in a deviation from classic rigs.

A small cabin aft, near the tiller, permitted Brenton to sit on deck

164

holding the tiller, with legs and feet inside the cabin. In rough seas, a plastic sheet placed across his knees warded off the water. Grub, tools, gear, clothing, cameras, typewriter, etc., were wrapped in plastic bags and stowed in the narrow inner hull, the bottom of which served as tight sleeping quarters. The craft, without the encumbrances of galley, heating devices, or system of illumination, was rigged with the help of expert canoeists and craftsmen: Austin Doe, Ralph Frese, and Richard E. Friedman.

The long adventure began on June 6, 1967, from Diversey Harbor, Chicago. Brenton proceeded across Lake Michigan and Lake Huron to the rapidly widening St. Lawrence River, where fog, tidal conditions, heavy surface chop, and danger of being run down by ocean liners menaced his trip before he reached the Atlantic Ocean. With its supposed favorable winds, the ocean was expected to carry the frail craft to Africa. But once he was on it, as the days melted into weeks, and weeks merged into months, the capricious tradewinds buffeted the canoe into a crazy course that threatened Brenton's destination—and dream.

Bucking strong headwinds and high waves, losing time and direction—for now navigational instruments were lost—Brenton was forced to sail by dead reckoning. After his radio failed, he plotted time from the sunset and sunrise, and then attempted to locate his position by using a nautical almanac. The near-swamping waves, hitting with a thud, were a constant threat, for only six inches of freeboard contributed to Brenton's slim margin of safety.

Brenton had constantly to contend with a rudder loosened by sharks and whales, with a diminishing supply of food and water, with wrists ringed with festering sores, with skin rubbed raw, with 26 consecutive hours at the helm. In the tradition of the sea, Brenton was provisioned with food and water from passing ships in several instances. It was during these meetings that he learned of disheartening errors in navigation; but he returned to the tiller and hoped that the southeastern winds would fill his sails and take him to Africa. Again, alone on the vastness of the sea, he pursued his destiny: sewing, seaming sails, adding new bracings and more nails to the rudder, devising methods of capturing birds and fish for food, at intervals surviving on the meager bounty of barnacles, eelgrass, and plankton.

The saga ended on November 30, 168 days after he left Chicago, when, 30 miles from the African beach, the Russian ship *Kostroma* forcibly hoisted the *Sierra Sagrada* aboard and a few days later set Brenton adrift again, within sight of Agadir—the objective won!

EXPO '67 VOYAGEUR CANOE PAGEANT

Participants in the pageant represented the elite of present-day canoeists in a spectacular race across the Dominion, from Rocky Mountain House, Alberta, to Montreal, Quebec, site of the Centennial celebration.

The modern voyageurs (trappers, miners, accountants, clerks, lawyers, students, railroaders) came from the shores of all the oceans bordering Canada, and from every province in between, to commemorate the colorful and courageous pioneer canoeists who opened water routes into Canada's interiors, linking the Atlantic, Pacific, and Arctic oceans, and who helped develop the land.

Ten teams (representing eight provinces and the two territories), in 25-foot double-ended canoes (replicas of the earlier craft), each named after a famous explorer in Canadian history, raced across 3,283 miles. Each team comprised nine paddlers and a chief voyageur. Each day six men paddled the whole day, while their teammates moved along shore to the next camp. Underway, the chief, usually in the stern, was in charge. The crews camped out each night, and, except when being entertained by a community along the route, did their own cooking.

Mayor Helen Hunley of Rocky Mountain House, its 2,800 residents, and thousands of spectators heard the starting-gun blast of the Honorable Judy La Marsh as the pageant was launched. Day after day, in sunshine and storm, the intrepid canoeists paddled: across the plains of the prairies, the northern muskeg country, into the face of Manitoba's windswept lakes and the white water of the Laurentian Shield, across the Great Lakes, into the waters of the Ottawa Valley, then the home stretch of the mighty St. Lawrence River. The entire course was broken into laps, or sprints, and the elapsed time for each lap was calculated and accumulated. The crew with the least elapsed time when reaching Montreal was declared winner.

One hundred and four paddling days later, the competitors arrived at Expo '67, with the three western provinces taking top honors. Manitoba took an early lead and was never headed—the elapsed time was 531 hours, 6 minutes, and 15½ seconds; British Columbia finished in second place, with 532 hours, 26 minutes, and 14 seconds; and Alberta was third with 535 hours, 19 minutes, and 30 seconds.

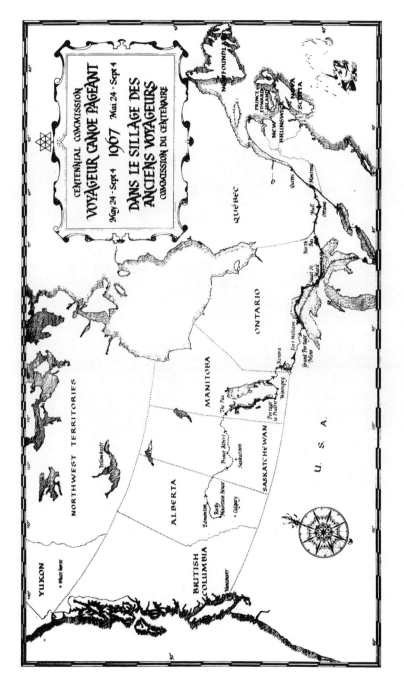

COMPETITIONS

Many country-wide canoe regattas, recreational and competitive, are staged annually by local business groups and canoe clubs, and this cross section is, of necessity, brief.

Launching the Manitoba canoe after an overnight stop, this crew went on to win the 3,283-mile Voyageur Canoe Pageant race from Rocky Mountain, Alberta, to Expo '67, Montreal. (CENTENNIAL COMMISSION OF CANADA)

A part of Flin Flon's (Manitoba) Annual Northern Festival, the Gold Rush Canoe Derby is a crowd-pleasing feature. Canoeists from Canada and the States competed (in 1968) for over $2,000 in prizes and trophies along an 80-mile stretch (in daily laps) of rivers, lakes, and portages in rough rugged forest in northern Manitoba and Saskatchewan, while trappers, fishermen, boaters, and tourists lined the shores to cheer. Amateurs raced over the same course for their championship.

The British Columbia crew paddles through rough waters to finish second in the Pageant race. (CENTENNIAL COMMISSION OF CANADA)

An annual 25-mile canoe marathon down the Des Plaines River, between Libertyville and Des Plaines, Illinois, is more than a long distance canoe race; it also attempts to alert the citizenry to water-pollution problems. The marathon, sponsored by the Illinois Paddling Council, includes divisions for Boys Scouts and boys, ages 11 to 13; Explorer Scouts and young men, 14 to 17; Girl Scouts and girls, 14 to 17; and categories for men 18 and over, women, mixed, and racing.

The Kentucky River Canoe Club co-sponsors with the University of Kentucky (Co-operative Extension Service) the Barren River Canoe Marathon, which provides competition for paddlers and excitement for spectators. The Barren River makes an ideal race course, as its water level is kept fairly constant by the Barren River Reservoir. The race events at Beech Bend Park cover many categories: boys, girls, men, women, mixed tandem, marathon, and men's cruising.

A canoe-packing contest is one of many events during the three-day festival held each February at The Pas in northern Manitoba. See Chapter 9 on *Transporting and Portaging the Canoe* for the details of this one-man overhead carry. (CANADIAN GOVERNMENT TRAVEL BUREAU)

The annual Texas Water Safari represents a rugged challenge—a 410-mile non-stop river run on the San Marcos and Guadalupe rivers. The competition is open to craft of any description as long as they are powered by hand—paddles, oars, or poles. Teams range from two to six, with no age limit, except that minors must present a waiver from parent or guardian. There is an entry fee of $50.00, and prizes total up to $6,500. If interested, write: Texas Safari, Box 721, San Marcos, Tex.

The annual California International Sea Festival, at Long Beach, shows an increasing popularity in paddling competitions. Standard and Olympic class canoes and kayaks share the program with rowing shells and outrigger canoes in events designed to dramatize the many watersports facilities of the southern California area. The Long Beach Marine Stadium, representing one of the finest competition courses in the world for paddling and rowing, is also used for the Olympic Canoe Trials. Director Skip Skibicki, with volunteers, hosts many regattas, as well as the American Canoe Association's Southwestern States Paddling Championships.

Canoe competition for the expert is available to test his increasing degree of efficiency, stamina, and excellence. Complete and up-to-date coverage of such competitions as the National, North American, Interscholastic Championships, and the Olympics, the top of the ladder, is available from the American Canoe Association (See "Organizations," below, for address) and its official organ, the *American Canoeist* magazine, published quarterly, at a subscription rate of $2.00 for one year, $3.00 for two years. Through the various editors—paddling, cruising, sailing, safety, and conservation—all aspects of the canoeing sport are encompassed. Through its regional divisions throughout the United States, the Association keeps the canoeist apprised of all coming events.

ACTIVITIES

In 1675, Father Jacques Marquette, S.J., celebrated the first Christian service to the Indians, on the bank of the Illinois River at the site of present-day Starved Rock State Park. Exactly 293 years later, on April 14, 1968, in tribute and reenactment, men, women, and children, dressed in period costumes, were borne by simulated birchbark craft and landed at the site of the simple altar. In the field setting with Indian tepees in the background, they heard Father Joseph P. Donnelly, also a Jesuit priest, celebrate the mass on an overturned canoe just as did his predecessor 293 years before. The participants in the historical celebration, led by Chairman Blaine Pool, included the Prairie Canoe Club, Illinois Paddling Council, many canoe enthusiasts, history buffs, and the Indian Center Club of Chicago.

171

The first crossing by canoe of the Okefenokee Swamp, Georgia, occurred over 30 years ago. In 1967, three of the original party members reenacted the feat. Mally Malinson and Harris Ball, members of the Seminole Canoe Club, and George Conley of the Royal Canoe Club, paddled through the seemingly interminable maze of trails of the swamp (now a wildlife refuge), of mysterious, overgrown, and unmapped water.

Regional canoe activities are too numerous to mention. Probably the most popular are those which center around the Sunday family or peer-group trips that include paddling, picnicking, and sightseeing. Everywhere that canoe groups flourish, you will find a local program of adventure.

An example of lighthearted, exuberant celebrating is the Yellowstone River Boat Float in July, when hundreds of tourists retrace the route of Lewis and Clark through southern Montana. Using anything that floats, including canoes, adventurers sail (in three daily laps) 135 miles down the rolling, rocky Yellowstone River, seeing scenery little changed from the time when Lewis and Clark saw it. All participants wear lifejackets, helicopters follow the flotilla, and many boats are outfitted with medical supplies. Meals, entertainment, and sleeping arrangements are handled by the Jaycees in each town, and some participants bring sleeping bags and tents (police guard campsites until dawn). This trip is reported to be of special appeal to children. Through 1968 no fee was charged. If interested, write Chamber of Commerce, Billings, Mont., where the float ends each year.

For the more ambitious canoeist, activity projects can include the retracing of famous routes: Canadian and stateside explorers, the Lewis and Clark expedition up the Missouri River, cruising down the length of the Mississippi, exploring the canal systems, or rediscovering that local historical route near your home.

ORGANIZATIONS

The canoe, after serving man for centuries, became a craft for recreation and competition over a hundred years ago. John MacGregor, a British lawyer, cruised many European rivers. As early as 1849, the interest generated led to the formation of the Royal Canoe Club on the Thames River, near London. The American Canoe Association, as a national organization, followed in 1880. Today ACA is an active organization with regional divisions throughout the country.

The local unorganized activities of canoeing, as practiced by weekend enthusiasts, fishermen, Boy Scouts, summer campers, and wilderness cruisers, number in the millions. Individual canoeists can be found on nearly every stream and lake, sometimes combining with other enthusiasts to form small regional clubs. Instruction in all the phases of canoeing is readily available at the numerous national aquatic schools conducted annually by the American Red Cross Water Safety Service, at summer camps, and at local park districts.

This list, acknowledged to be incomplete, will serve the canoeist, even in the most remote section of the country, to launch or expand his adventure.

THE AMERICAN CANOE ASSOCIATION has the purpose of encouraging recreational canoeing—from short weekend trips to the extensive camping-cruises of long distances and duration. It is concerned with the sponsorship of national paddling and sailing competition, and with competition with the Canadian Canoe Association. According to Theodore G. Alteneder, Jr., ACA's representative on the United States Olympic Board of Directors, the Association nominates seven of the nine members of the Olympic Canoeing and Kayaking Committee. This committee's efforts are toward fund-raising, team development, selection, and final training—all aspects of the preparation of the canoeing team. The National Paddling Committee has full responsibility for setting up and conducting the Olympic Trials. (Doris C. C. Cousins, Secretary, 400 Eastern St., New Haven, Conn. 06513.)

CANADIAN CANOE ASSOCIATION, c/o Frank Clement, Secretary, 3210 St. Joseph Boulevard, Lachine, Quebec, Canada.

THE AMERICAN WHITEWATER CLUB is a federation of over 50 white-water clubs in North America, as well as having individual members. It publishes a quarterly magazine, *American White Water*. Membership and magazine for $2.50 annually. Write: Robert Hawley, 1925 Hopkins St., Berkeley, Calif. 94707.

AMERICAN YOUTH HOSTELS (main office at 20 W. 17th Street, New York, N.Y. 10011), a non-profit, non-sectarian, non-political corporation, is open to all who subscribe to its principles. Its expressed purpose is to foster outdoor activities, educational and recreational travel, creative group programs; to develop healthy, happy, self-reliant, well-informed citizens, and to provide youth hostels—simple overnight accommodations in scenic, historical, and cultural areas, with supervising house parents and local sponsorship. Membership is open to both sexes: ages 9 to 94 are eligible to join. Canoeing is gaining many adherents among hostelers.

AMERICAN RED CROSS sponsors small craft schools, basic canoeing courses, instructor-training rescue operations, safety first, etc. Contact your local chapter.

UNITED STATES CANOE ASSOCIATION, a newly formed Midwest canoeing group, is designed to fill a void which existed in the definition and organization of cruising-canoe competition. Charles Moore, 6338 Hoover Rd., Indianapolis, Ind. 46260.

WISCONSIN HOOFERS OUTING CLUB membership is limited to students and faculty of the University of Wisconsin; however, non-members who have their own equipment can arrange to join club trips by writing to: Secretary, Wisconsin Hoofers Outing Club, Memorial Union, University of Wisconsin, Madison 53706.

THE KEEPOTAW CANOE CLUB is organized for the teaching of competitive paddling. Its members participate in both long-distance marathon races and the Olympic canoe and kayak races all over the Midwest. Write: Lynn Tuttle, 127 Division St., St. Charles, Ill. 60174.

AMERICAN INDIAN CENTER CANOE CLUB is one of the unique canoe clubs in the nation, devoted to competitive canoeing and cruising. It sponsors a yearly race on Lake Michigan called "Day She Shek" ("Bad Water"). Write Leroy Wesaw, 2209 N. Campbell, Chicago, Ill. 60647.

THE LINCOLN PARK BOAT CLUB is the only boat club on Lake Michigan with facilities for rowing and paddling for both competition and pleasure. It has boat storage facilities and is situated at the end of Fullerton Avenue, in Chicago. Write Frank Dallos, Secretary, 2236 N. Burling, Chicago, Ill. 60614, or J. Joseph, Director, 626 Rice St., Highland Park, Ill. 60035.

20

Mapping the Adventure: Water Trails and Map Sources

WATER TRAILS

Canoe trails in the United States and Canada range from ponds to wild stretches of white water. As canoeists refine their skills, the inexhaustible waters of the North American continent beckon the enthusiast to a lifetime of enjoyment.

The traditional canoe country—Canada, the Adirondacks of New York and New England, Maine, Michigan, Wisconsin, and Minnesota—has been enlarged by the burgeoning number of weekend and vacationing devotees to include practically every state of the Union and every province of Canada. In true voyageur spirit, modern canoeists continually discover new challenges and enlarge the boundaries of their adventures.

It is impossible to list all canoeing waters. We shall indicate some sources that will make it easier to find accessible waters within the ranges of one's abilities and resources.

Canada

Canada was first explored, then developed, through its unique waterways system: one-half of the world's fresh water is within its boundaries! It is possible to paddle a canoe from practically any Canadian city to the Atlantic, Pacific, or Arctic oceans, or to the Gulf of Mexico.

The Hudson's Bay Company, with posts scattered throughout the dominion, offers in its U-Paddle Canoe Rental Service a program that is new in wilderness outfitting. Canoes for a trip are picked up at one Company post, paddled to distant posts, and dropped off without backtracking—very similar to the operation of U-Drive cars, trucks, and trailers. At this writing, the posts (with more to be included) engaged in the program are: Yellowknife, Waterways, Ile à la Crosse, La Ronge, and Norway House. Grub supply fill-ins and general briefings are supplied by the post manager to launch the modern-day voyageur on his wilderness adventure. Just visiting and observing the Hudson's Bay enterprise (dating back to 1670) will be a thrilling experience. Inquire: The Northern Stores Department, Hudson's Bay Company, Winnipeg, Canada.

ALGOMA SECTION of ONTARIO. This wilderness area, northeast of Lake Superior, is a roadless region whose interior is penetrated by the Algoma Central Railway out of Sault Ste. Marie ("the Soo"). The railroad—originally used by lumberjacks, trappers, and miners, and now popular with fisherman, hunters, and canoeists—for 299 miles remains a frontier train, running north into wild country. The scenery is of rugged beauty: the Montreal River plunging and racing toward Lake Superior, Agawa Canyon with its pine-hung bluffs and a raging river below. Bridal Veil Falls and several others in lacy sheets of white water plunge into the canyon below. The first part of the route, from the Soo to Hawk Junction, is trout water, while the route from Hawk Junction to Hearst—the end of the line—is known for its walleye and northern fishing. The daily train drops off canoeists at any one of the ten major rivers along the way, for trips of a few days or weeks. When you are tired or finished with your trip, you need make no prearrangement—simply carry the canoe and duffle to the railroad siding, stack them, flag down the train, and board!

The Algoma rivers weave to and from the railroad, and a variety of trips are available. One, neither rough nor hazardous, is the Hilda-Michipicoten trip, which takes the canoe party through plenty of wild country without too many portages or too much white water.

Your adventure train leaves at 7:00 A.M. daily except Sundays. An early arrival is recommended for safe railroad parking-lot parking of your car for the duration of your trip and for canoe and duffle to be tagged and loaded.

176

For timetable, brochure, and answers to your trip questions, write: Traffic Manager, Algoma Central Railway, Sault Ste. Marie, Ontario, Canada.

ALGONQUIN PROVINCIAL PARK, ONTARIO. Set aside exclusively for canoe-camping, this is a vast 3,000-square-mile wilderness of sparkling water and virgin forests, less than 300 miles from the United States border. Each year, over 5,000 canoeists (80 per cent of them from the States) visit the park. Approximate driving distances to the provincial park from some cities in the States are: Buffalo, 261 miles; Cleveland, 450 miles; Detroit, 396 miles; New York, 517 miles; Philadelphia, 544 miles; and Pittsburgh, 481 miles.

The park, virtually unscarred by roads, offers a sanctuary of clean water and virgin trees, where wildlife thrives in an unspoiled environment. On the back trails, canoeists can observe beaver, deer, moose, and bear. As many as 116 species of birds are known to nest in the park. On some of the 2,100 lakes within the park, canoeists can go days without seeing another party; and the portages offer little problem, as the lakes and connecting streams are close together.

It is almost impossible to get lost in the park's waters, so well marked are the maps. However, aircraft patrol the park daily, in case someone should get lost and not return on schedule.

The Algonquin Outfitters, under the direction of woods-wise natives, can supply all your needs, from canoe to waterproof matches. Should you be away from Algonquin and not wish to be burdened with freighting canoe and duffle, less than $8.00 per person, per day, will pay for all your needs.

Prince Philip and his royal party visited the park in 1959, canoed to a remote lake, and brought out 40 lake trout. People of all ages, from all walks of life, enjoy the "royal" canoeing and fishing advantages of the Algonquin preserve.

Ontario, with its 250,000 lakes, is a canoeing paradise. Over a thousand miles lie between the Rideau Lake District in eastern Ontario and the Lake of the Woods at the western boundary; in almost every square mile of that area there is a lake, a stream, or a river in which the canoe can be used. The same is true of most Canadian provinces.

Canada's wealth of woods and waters defies the imagination. It is possible to cross Canada by canoe, and one sees as much of the clean country as in 1613, when Samuel de Champlain paddled its waterways in search of a gateway to the Orient.

Each province willingly extols its virtues. Select your Eden, and write for information, stating your needs (definitely and in detail), and if possible give the particular section of the province in which you are interested, to receive:

"Prince Edward Island Canoeing," The Prince Edward Island Travel Bureau, Charlottetown, P.E.I.

"Water Trails of Nova Scotia," Department of Publicity, Halifax, N.S.

"Cruising in New Brunswick," Government Bureau of Travel Information, Fredericton, N.B.

"Quebec Waterways," Quebec Tourist Bureau, Quebec City, P.Q.

"Ontario Lakes and Streams," Department of Travel and Publicity, Parliament Building, Toronto.

"With Canoe and Paddle in Manitoba," Bureau of Travel and Publicity, Winnipeg, Manitoba.

"Interesting Saskatchewan Trips," the Saskatchewan Tourist Buildings, Regina, Saskatchewan.

"Canoeing in Alberta," Alberta Travel Bureau, Edmonton, Alberta.

"British Columbia's Scenic Routes," The British Columbia Travel Bureau, Victoria, B.C.

CANADIAN RAILROADS. The canoe and the railroad in Canada, a compatible combination from earliest times, served the discovery and development of the continent. Their kinship remains, for the canoeist with his craft and duffle uses the train to extend the scope of his canoeing range. These railroads, serving their respective regions, supply information:

Canadian National Railways, Montreal, P.Q.

Canadian Pacific Railway, Montreal, P.Q.

Dominion Atlantic Railway, Halifax, N.S.

Ontario Northland Railway, North Bay, Ontario

Algoma Central Railway, Sault Ste. Marie, Ontario

BUSH PLANES provide accessibility to remote canoeing waters by flying in canoe and gear. Bush-plane pilots transport your canoe on the undercarriage of their planes, and are reliable and safe—though sometimes, when they are coming out of the bush carrying a delicate cargo of spoilable fish, the canoeist may drop in priority. Thanks to bush pilots, no water is denied the canoeist; there is no such thing as an inaccessible chain of lakes or river course when you engage fly-in service.

THE CANADIAN GOVERNMENT TRAVEL BUREAU, 150 Kent St., Ottawa, Ontario, and the Ontario Department of Tourism and Information, 185 Bloor St. East, Toronto, Ontario, will furnish air-service listings, maps, and general information. The Travel Bureau also has free literature, provided by the provinces, including booklets: "Firearms and Fishing Tackle," general regulations governing entry and transportation in each of the provinces and Territories, including a complete list of the Provincial Travel Bureaus in Canada, which will answer questions on regulations, licenses, fishing conditions, etc.; and "Canada Border Crossing Information." The Canadian Government Travel Bureau maintains offices in the States in Boston, Chicago, Cincinnati, Cleveland, Detroit, Hartford, Indianapolis, Los Angeles, Minneapolis, New York, Philadelphia, Pittsburgh, Rochester, San Francisco, Seattle, and Washington, D.C.

The crew of the Ontario entry in the Expo '67 Canoe Pageant tunes up in a ten-day trial race held before the pageant. The race started at Fort St. James and ended at Victoria, British Columbia. The 25-foot canoes were replicas of the voyageur canoes used to explore and settle Canada. (CENTENNIAL COMMISSION OF CANADA)

United States

Canoeing in the States has expanded in recent years to include practically every state—southern, prairie, mountain, and coastal. Various departments in most states have mapped canoe trails through scenic

179

and historical areas, cleared portage paths and stream obstructions, and delineated campsites to lure the canoeist. In each state canoeing is different; in all it is adventurous!

CALIFORNIA, known throughout the world for its scores of state beaches, parks, preserves, recreation areas, 19 fishing areas, 11 national parks, 11 national forests, and 18 reclamation lakes, adds up to unexcelled leisure-time possibilities.

The brochure, "California State Park System," from Department of Parks and Recreation, P.O. Box 2390, Sacramento, Calif. 95811, lists them all.

Canoeing is enjoyed on many inland waters. McArthur-Burney Falls State Park, with a twin waterfall 129 feet high, camp and picnic sites, is one of the state's best. Fishing for trout, bass, bluegills, and catfish offers an added bonus.

The heavily wooded shores and a meandering river give Woodson Bridge Recreation Area a beauty all its own. As you cruise, fish for salmon, steelhead, and trout.

Brannon Island gives access to fabulous delta fishing, as well as to an exploration of the back sloughs of the Sacramento River and angling for bluegills and crappies.

Donner Memorial State Park is a mountain jewel; lake and creek combine to give a canoeing experience in high, thin atmosphere. And besides lakes of high elevation, the canoeist in California can cruise in the lowest water in the States—234 feet below sea level—at Salton Sea. Salt-water fish, such as croaker, mullet, corvina, and sargo thrive in this unique body of water.

Millerton Lake, created by Friant Dam which backs up the San Joaquin River, is a popular spot. Its 30 campsites are accessible only to boaters who must navigate upstream to them.

Canoeing on water with desert country reaching as far as the eye can see is possible only in California. The Colorado River, 23 miles north of Winterhaven, in the Picacho Recreation Area, is a place where this can be done. It offers canoeing, camping, and picnicking.

FLORIDA is beginning to discover its vast canoeing potential. With thousands of navigable lakes and rivers, it offers unlimited opportunities for pleasure cruising, exciting exploration, and superb fishing. The northern rivers—Apalachicola, St. Johns, and the Suwannee River, originating in the Okefenokee Swamp in Georgia and flowing through exotic land to the Gulf of Mexico above Cedar Key—represent the upper part of the state.

The Caloosahatchee River to the south makes possible a cross-state

180

trip from Fort Myers on the Gulf, through Lake Okeechobee, to the Atlantic Ocean.

In between these areas lie many clear streams, spring-fed and sporty, for example, the Withlacoochee, Rainbow, Crystal, Homosassa, Chassahowitzka, Indian, St. Lucie, Anclote, Kissimmee, Charley, Myakka, Manatee, and many others.

The many large rivers and lakes (used by many motorized craft) with changing wind conditions require caution on the part of the canoeist.

The Withlacoochee, Suwannee, and Kissimmee Rivers are among America's few remaining unspoiled rivers, coursing through the least explored areas of the state. The wild stretches of land in Florida, the national forests and state parks, combine to make cruising unique: orchids on stream banks, palm-fringed woodlands, and tunnels of overhanging vegetation.

Inquire of the American Camping Association, Florida section, E. M. Schmidt, Bradford Woods, Martinsville, Ind. 46151, regarding "Canoe Trips in Florida." Both the Publicity Division of the Florida Development Commission and the Board of Parks and Historic Monuments are at 101 W. Gaines St., Tallahassee, Fla. 32301.

GEORGIA's primeval swamplands, sparkling lakes, fields, and streams, lush with nature's flora and fauna, provide a soul-satisfying pilgrimage to precolonial days. Some mountain streams, like those near Dahlonega and Mount Crown, offer gold-panning possibilities, and rock-hounding, too, is practiced in the rocky stream beds. Okefenokee Swamp, the "land of trembling earth," is in Georgia, and some parts of it are unexplored to this day, offering a rare challenge in adventure for the canoeist (see Florida).

Write: Georgia Department of Industry and Trade, 100 State Capitol, Atlanta, Georgia 30334; for additional information, to Department of State Parks, 7 Hunter St., S.W., Atlanta.

ILLINOIS. The "Illinois Canoeing Guide," obtainable from the Illinois Department of Conservation, 400 S. Spring St., Springfield, Ill. 62700, shows the rich tradition of canoe travel along Illinois canoe watercourses. Its streams knew the paddles of Cartier, Joliet, LaSalle, Marquette, and many voyageurs. Today, the same trails are enjoyed by many canoe groups in ever-increasing numbers.

Along the Illinois water trails, the canoeist can visit Little Grand Canyon to find one of the few remaining truly wilderness areas of the state. In the "Land of Lincoln," he can cruise Salt Fork River, along which runs a state road traveled by Abraham Lincoln in his judicial circuit.

Write to Jack Johnson, 12 N. Cottonhill, Springfield, Ill. 62700, regarding his "Lincoln Heritage Canoe Trail (Sangamon River)."

The primitive Spoon River, whose name is familiar because of Edgar Lee Masters' *Spoon River Anthology,* is spanned by the historic covered Wolf Bridge, an excellent place to embark, to take-out, to camp, or to fish.

On the western bank of the Wabash River, near Mount Carmel, is Beall Woods, a 625-acre tract of virgin trees, unsurpassed in the variety of species—some up to 160 feet in height. One 400-year-old red oak is the oldest oak in the United States.

Illinois rivers, with field, cliff, or wooded banks, enable the canoeist to cruise for 76 miles on the Pecatonica, 130 miles on the Embarras, 150 on the Rock, and for 272 miles on the Illinois to its juncture with the Mississippi.

The Saline River takes the canoeist through a bygone era—when the population density was greater than that of Chicago. There are the Batavia Bog, fossils, and cypress swamps (for those interested in scientific aspects of canoeing), huge stands of virgin woods, cliffs as high as 300 feet, and the rare pileated woodpecker to see.

Write: The Chicagoland Canoe Base, Ralph C. Frese, 4019 N. Narragansett, Chicago, Ill. 60634, for information on "The Historic Fox Valley Canoe Trail."

Canoeists in the Chicagoland region, boasting many paddling organizations—Great Lakes Chapter of the Sierra Club, Prairie Club Canoeists, American Youth Hostels, Illinois Paddling Council, Chicagoland Canoe Base, and Scout groups—are constantly finding nearby streams that bring the joy of discovery and add new potential canoeing horizons.

INDIANA. Trip information and a map, "Canoe Trails in Indiana," are available from the Department of Natural Resources, Division of Water, Indianapolis, Ind. 46204. Information on "Pigeon River Canoe Trail" is available from Area Manager, Pigeon River Conservation Area, R.R. #2, Howe, Ind. 46746.

The number of canoes car-topped and traveling over the Indiana highways has risen steadily in the past few years, for canoeists have discovered secluded rivers and streams, away from the pressures of cities. They are unconcerned about four-barrel carburetors, launching difficulties, or the nearest source of gasoline, for they have learned that the peace and serenity found in natural settings is satisfying to the soul.

Families, large groups, Scout troops, and canoe clubs float on one of the 16 rivers for varied activity that ranges from bow-and-arrow fishing to ducking under historic covered bridges. Add an Indiana stream to your collection of canoe adventures—take your pick from the Fawn River trip of 20 miles through two counties, to the Wabash River across counties too numerous to mention, and you will absorb some Hoosier humor, philosophy, and hospitality.

IOWA. Through the canoe trails of Iowa ("Canoe Trips," Iowa Conservation Commission, East 7th and Court, Des Moines, Iowa), you will come to know and realize the adventure of early explorers and settlers, who came through the state during the Louisiana Purchase era of the 1800's.

The guide contains, along with a complete description of its many canoe trips, scaled maps, well-defined landmarks, and intriguing bits of history. For example, Old Bone's Mill, built in 1854, had a colorful past, with its continual battle with ice and flood waters, its business function, a dash of romance, even a murder, which today remains unsolved. There are also the mystery along the Boone River below Bell's Mill, where a cave entrance, with its fallen-away steps, lures the explorer to seek the solution of the mystery—still unsolved—of a fabulous treasure; Boneyard Hollow, where Indians drove buffalo, deer, and elk from the adjacent prairies over the cliffs to their death for meat and furs; Mormon Ridge, where many unmarked graves give evidence of the Mormon tragedy during the winter of 1844-45. In the Mormons' westward migration, they camped on the South Fork of the Iowa River as harsh weather set in, and underwent suffering and death from exposure, cold, and lack of provisions. And there are caves in the sandstone cliffs which Jesse James supposedly used as a hideout.

The "Iowa Canoe Trips" booklet is replete with such interesting background material, and there's a story in each river: the Boone, Des Moines, Iowa, Little Sioux, Raccoon, Volga, Rock, Turkey, Red Cedar, Yellow, and Wapsipinicon. Many are typical prairie streams, shallow, meandering, best navigated by the canoe. The waterways necessitate a minimum of portages. They offer delightful slow cruising, which enables the canoeist to absorb the views of lush growth, broad valleys, ravines, towering sandstone walls, gorges rich in Indian lore, and mineral substances from the copperas family whose powder the Indians used for war paint and fabric coloring.

KANSAS, where water is a way of life—and what a life for the prairie dweller! One looks at the map, available from its State Fish and Game Department, Box F, Pratt, Kans. 67124, and discovers that practically every county is dotted or streaked with a creek, stream, farm pond, strip-mine pit, river, lake, or reservoir.

The booklet, "Where to Fish in Kansas," from the Forestry Commission, Box 1028, Pratt, Kans. 67124, lists the state's water resources (alphabetically and regionally). The large rivers include the Arkansas, Big and Little Blue, Cimarron, Cottonwood, Marais des Cygnes, Neosho, Republican, Saline, and a few others. These waters invite long canoe cruises, and offer catfish havens as a bonus. Flatheads weighing 60 to 70 pounds have been captured.

The water level of rivers is an important consideration in Kansas, and should be checked before embarking on long trips. The eastern two-thirds of the state contain the spring-fed watercourses that differ in character from the others.

Another source of Kansas information is Travel Division, Kansas Department of Economic Development, State Office Building, Topeka, Kansas.

KENTUCKY. Roam through history as you canoe in Kentucky. Landmarks and state parks honor such famous Americans as Daniel Boone, George Rogers Clark, John James Audubon, and Abraham Lincoln. Most of the state has canoeing possibilities, though no prescribed routes are published by the Kentucky Department of Public Information, Capitol Annex, Frankfort, Ky. 40601. There are 12 major impoundments, 41 state-owned lakes, and big rivers with more miles of running water than any other state except Alaska—offering a year-round canoeing program.

Probably the five best canoeing streams for the adventurous canoeist are today not too different from the wilds that Daniel Boone knew. Few have seen these areas, and that's enough challenge for the canoeist. The streams, off the beaten path, offer one- to five-day trips in which not a single house, farm, or man will be seen: (1) the North, Middle, and South Forks of the Kentucky River; (2) Cumberland River in the far eastern part of the Kentucky Mountains; (3) Green River; (4) Red River; and (5) Licking River.

Many smaller streams, scenic mountain lakes, and state parks along with the "Land Between the Lakes," a wildlife area of 60,000 acres between Kentucky and Barkley Lakes, add up to a canoeing bonanza for Kentuckians and tourists alike. The State Department of Parks is at Frankfort.

MAINE offers 28 choice views of nature available only to the canoeist, and lists them in "Maine Canoeing," available through the Department of Economic Development, Gateway Circle, Portland, Me. 04102.

A description of the canoe trip reveals the state's premier status: a short trip on the West Branch of the Penobscot River has few peers in the variety of water, scenic charms, and good fishing. Canoeists return year after year to find new streams to explore, new wonders, new fishing spots, and new beautiful campsites which charm the canoe-campers to linger for days. The East Branch of the Penobscot, in its wild race of 118 miles, is rough enough to test the artistry and skill of the most seasoned canoeist.

Canoeists paddling in perfect rhythm in New England whitewater. Note the pole they have cut for use in situations where poling will be the most effective means of propulsion. (OLD TOWN CANOE CO.)

The Allagash Lake trip includes the sights of deep forests, where deer and moose feed at the water's edge, miles of quick water, water-falls of dazzling beauty, caves and caverns, small lakes, and lazy backwaters.

The 201-mile St. Johns River trip is the longest and most difficult offered by the state. The three-week (suggested time) canoe trip takes the adventurer through the wildest part of Maine, where game is plentiful and unafraid, and canoe-handling skills constantly are being tested.

The Moose Lake trip lists the variety of experiences available on one body of water. One can explore bays, coves, outlets, islands, and Mt. Kineo.

The Rangely Lakes trip, in high country (1,200 feet), offers superb scenic views, with ideal fishing and a minimum of carries.

An entire summer of canoeing adventure is possible on the Grand Lake-Machias River trip, if one adopts the unhurried pace of nature.

There are many ways the trip can be implemented—extended layovers, side trips on lakes and streams off the main route, exploration, hiking—to guarantee a delightful summer.

The "Maine Guide" is a legendary figure in canoe-tripping lore, and acquaintance with Maine's waters immediately reveals the necessity of using experienced help for certain waters. The guide, like the outfitter, is an important resource person for both novice and veteran canoeist.

NEW ENGLAND STATES. Comprehensive canoe-trail information for the northeastern states is in the "New England Canoeing Guide," available for $5.00 from Appalachian Mountain Club, 5 Joy St., Boston, Mass. 02108.

MICHIGAN touts itself as a "Water Wonderland," and with its 36,000 miles of rivers and streams, it can truly be called a "Canoeing Wonderland." At every major crossroad in parts of the state, there are stacks of wood-canvas and aluminum canoes for rent—by gas stations, grocery, hardware, and sporting goods stores.

"Canoe Trails of Michigan," Michigan Tourist Council, 114 S. Walnut St., Lansing, Mich. 48933, is a pocket-sized guide with many pointers for both expert and novice canoeists. All canoe trips are carefully described, and a clearly defined map shows the location of 44 canoe adventures.

The rivers of the Upper Peninsula draining into Lake Superior are wild streams with numerous falls, rocky chasms, and deep woods—unpopulated by man. These canoe trails of fast water through rugged country are mainly for the expert canoeist, who is rewarded for his proficiency by being able to explore remote places, and enjoy spectacular scenery and fabulous fishing.

The Tahquamenon River, fringed with virgin trees, is Hiawatha country, with deer, bear, ducks, osprey, eagles, trout, bass, and pike.

Rugged river trips in the Upper Peninsula include: Presque Isle, Ontonagon, Paint, Net, Michigamme, Menominee, and the Escanaba.

In east and west Michigan, the waterways are equally alluring for the canoeist. Again, the profusion of woods, the land contour, the clean water threading through unpopulated areas, give a wide range for adventure. Popular streams that offer campsites, cleared portage paths, and outfitters, include the Boardman, Au Sable, Big Manistee, Pine, Little Manistee, Pere Marquette, Muskegon, Grand, Thornapple, Kalamazoo, Brule, Black, Paw Paw, St. Joseph, Tittibawasee, and Huron.

MINNESOTA. The Superior-Quetico canoe country, including the Superior National Forest in Minnesota, and Quetico Provincial Park in Ontario, Canada—without comparison on the continent—is probably the most popular with stateside canoeists (over 100,000 each year, possibly 25,000 for the first time). The vast wilderness of 14,500 square miles enables the canoe-camper to spend a day or a month in the land of the voyageurs, accessible only by canoe and pack. Since 1909, when the Canadian portion was set aside as Quetico Provincial Park and the American area as the Superior National Forest, the countries have combined to preserve the inseparable unit of interlacing waterways as it had been in the days of Radisson and Groseilliers, who explored the region in 1660.

Should you wish to enter the Quetico and be outfitted on the Canadian side, write Kawene Chamber of Commerce, or Department of Lands and Forests, both in Toronto, Canada.

Families, Scouts, college and high-school youths take to this land of connecting water trails for trips of days, weeks, or months. So extensive is the sky-blue water that there is no backtracking. The day's cruise ended, the canoeists camp on a pine-needle carpet, often frying over an open fire the tasty trout, pike, or bass readily caught in this finest fishing water in the Midwest.

There's a deep wilderness solitude in Superior-Quetico: unspoiled, litter-free, clean, and without cabins, docks, resorts, or other evidences of civilization. It remains as it was in the days of the voyageurs, and through reading their diaries, the modern canoeist can duplicate their routes and experiences.

A complete atlas of the entire Superior-Quetico area can be purchased from W. A. Fisher Co., Virginia, Minn. 55792, for $2.50.

There are three main push-off areas, with excellent outfitting available, to the interior of the Quetico. For information and interesting reading, write: The Gunflint Trail Association, Grand Marais, Minn. 55604; The Ely Commercial Club, Ely, Minn. 55731; The Crane Lake Commercial Club, Crane Lake, Minn. 55725.

In addition to the three access points from Minnesota into the Superior-Quetico canoe country, there are many little-known rivers that provide canoeing opportunities. Equal to or better than those of any area in North America is their claim.

There are many lakes threaded with rivers over the entire state: the Rum, Crow Wing, Straight, Root, Blackhoof, to name a few. An excellent little-used route is the Red Lake River which follows a crooked course of scenic terrain through the Red Lake Indian Reservation.

Canoeists should first inquire about possible hazards and water conditions on little-known rivers. The canoe waterways in Minnesota, challenging but navigable, are so plentiful that it is impossible to list all of them.

"Little-Known Minnesota Rivers Great for Canoeing," and "Wilderness Canoe Trips," mimeographed information sheets, are available from: Visitor Information Center, Department of Economic Development, 57 West 7th St., St. Paul, Minn. 55102.

For information on "Wilderness Crow Wing Canoe Trail," write: John E. Rife, Chairman, Crow Wing Canoe Trail Committee, Box 210, Sebeka, Minn. 56477.

MISSOURI. The scenic riverways of the Missouri Ozarks represent a "land of dreams as old as time itself." The sand and pebbled stream beds, crystal-clear water flowing from numerous springs, running through green, forest-covered mountains, in a majesty that has withstood time, remain today as when the Indians and the pioneers floated on them.

If names like Bee Bluff, Ebb and Flow Spring, Buck Hollow, Jam Up Cave, and Legendary Lost Cave stir your bloodstream and haunt your mind, then buy (for $1.50) the "River Maps of the Current and Jack's Fork" locally or from the Map Shop, 10th and Olive Sts., St. Louis, Mo. 63102.

The state offers 16,000 miles of swift white water and spring-fed streams which make possible year-round adventure. Float fishing streams, ideal for canoeing, abound, and outfitters are numerous along Missouri's famous rivers. For the Big Piney River, information, outfitting, and canoe rental are available at the town of Licking; for the Bryant and North Fork, at Tecumseh; for the Current and Eleven Point, at Doniphan; for the Elk River, and Sugar and Indian creeks, at Noel; for the Gasconade, at Morrison; for the Meramec, Huzzah, and Courtois rivers, at Steelville; for Niangua River, at Bennett Springs and at Eldridge; and other Current and Jack's Fork references (mentioned earlier) are the towns of Alley Springs, Akers, Eminence, Gladden, and Round Spring.

State-wide canoeing information is available from: Eureka Valley Floats, 6347 N. Rosebury Ave., Clayton, Mo. 63105; Midwest Canoe Floats, 4109 Malcon, LeMay, Mo. 63125; and Ozark Canoe Rental Service, 614 Tuxedo Blvd., Webster Groves, Mo. 63019.

These references, along with other information, are available from the booklet, "Float Fishing Outfitters," Missouri State Division of Commerce and Industrial Development. Another source of information: "Missouri Ozark Waterways," Missouri Conservation Commission, both in Jefferson City, Mo. 65101.

NEW JERSEY. The historical and famous Delaware River—crossed by George Washington, source of water for many cities, running a distance of 200 miles—flows through New Jersey, New York, and Pennsylvania. Its entire course, from New York in the western Catskill Mountains, to Trenton, New Jersey, has been mapped in detail by the Delaware River Basin Commission. Ten two-color recreation maps, bound in booklet form, show the parks and forests that line the river. River characteristics, like rapids, riffles, and pools, depths, and streamflow are described and located. The maps are available for $1.00 prepaid, from the Delaware River Basin Commission, Box 360, Trenton, N.J. 08603.

Many groups trip along the historic Raritan Canal, between Bound Brook and Princeton, which takes the canoeists on a route that was heavily traveled before and after the Revolutionary War.

For additional canoeing possibilities, write: Conservation Department, 53 E. State St., Trenton, N.J. 08603; and see *Exploring the Little Rivers of New Jersey,* by James and Margaret Cawley (Rutgers University Press, New Brunswick, N.J. 04330).

NEW YORK. There are many short, inexpensive, quiet afternoon or weekend trips that are made to order for enjoyable family-type canoe experiences. For example, paddle Black Creek or Fall Stream on gentle currents, fishing for perch or bass. Scenic and historic runs, meadowlands that should intrigue the bird watcher and botanist, placid streams through pastoral country, all combine to soothe the harried dweller in crowded places.

To experience the interesting gamut of waterways in New York, try your paddle on the Sarnac River, with its rough water that challenges the canoeist's skill, or the Delaware River from Hancock to Callicoon— the favorite run of the American Canoe Association canoeists—which offers a real white-water challenge.

The 120-mile long chain of lakes in the state's Adirondack Forest Preserve offers canoeing within a few hours' driving time from any part of New York. Access points, cruising cautions on large lakes, availability of campsites, lean-tos, historical notes, permit information, and guides are in an all-inclusive pamphlet, "Adirondack Canoe Routes," by William G. Howard, M.F. It is available from State of New York, Conservation Department, Recreation Circular 7, Albany, N.Y. 12226. The information leaflet, "Canoe Trips," can be obtained from the same source.

Canoeable Waterways of New York State, by Lawrence I. Grinnell, has been published by Pageant Press, 130 W. 42nd St., New York 10036.

"OHIO Canoe Trails," is available from the Department of Natural

Resources, Division of Watercraft, 802 Ohio Departments Bldg., Columbus, Ohio.

PENNSYLVANIA. The Allegheny, Monongahela, Ohio, Susquehanna, and Delaware, famous historical rivers, are canoeable waters in the hemlock and mountain laurel state. As he cruises the varied water routes, the canoeist sees famous forts, remains of old barge canals, mines, wood dams, covered bridges, pastoral scenes, and varying degrees of wilderness, and he experiences varied stream challenges.

"Canoe Routes," from the Commonwealth of Pennsylvania, Department of Forests and Waters, Harrisburg, Pa., lists rivers in alphabetical order, and gauging-station locations, so that canoeists can check on the minimum reading of two feet, before embarking on the smaller rivers. Sources for local topographic maps are also included.

Streams have been given an approximate rating according to the skill required to navigate them. The rating system, applicable only to Pennsylvania, includes five categories: (*a*) no difficulties caused by the current; (*b*) occasional slight riffles, but these are very easy; (*c*) slightly stronger currents in the riffles, but no long or difficult passages—no difficulty to persons having any experience in handling a canoe; (*d*) more frequent riffles and larger rocks, but with ample opportunity for rescue in case of an upset; wearing of life jacket recommended; (*e*) only for the canoeist experienced in white-water skills—steeper drops, higher standing waves, trickier and longer rapids require frequent scouting from shore and may require lining through, or portaging around, difficult rapids.

A complete canoeing guide is being compiled by the Department. Up-to-date information is presently available from the American Youth Hostels, Inc., 6300 Fifth Ave., Pittsburgh, Pa. 15232.

For a complete guide to the Delaware River, write to the Delaware River Basin Commission, 25 Scotch Rd., Surburban Square, Trenton, N.J., for their "Regional Maps."

TENNESSEE. Write the Division of State Parks, Department of Conservation, 2611 West End Ave., Nashville, Tenn. 37203.

VIRGINIA. "Canoeing White Water in North Virginia and N. E. Virginia," by Randy Carter, is available from Louis Matacia, 3430 Lee Highway, Fairfax, Va. 22030. The Division of Parks, Southern State Bldg., Richmond, Va. 23219, will also answer queries.

WISCONSIN. Read "Canoe Trails of Wisconsin," available from the Wisconsin Conservation Department, Madison, Wisc. 53701, and select almost any type of paddling adventure. The Flambeau River Trail (Trip No. 24), with roaring rapids, wilderness scenery, and wildlife is one type. The Wisconsin River Trail (Trip No. 17), moving slowly, paralleling highways along some of its course, making it possible to use wayside tables and fireplaces, and to keep in touch with civilization —to make a phone call, to replenish your larder, or to buy a fishing lure—is its opposite.

The booklet lists 48 canoe trips, and includes detailed information

Tennessee's Big Ridge State Park, where year-round fishing is possible on a 45-acre lake stocked with bass and bluegill. Canoes are available for rent. (TENNESSEE DIVISION OF STATE PARKS)

on starting points, paddling time, portages, camp and fishing sites, etc. On Wisconsin rivers, streams, and lakes, canoeists see virgin timber— pine, hemlock, hardwood—and experience what the first canoeists in the state knew: good fishing in fast-running water below towering granite cliffs, and for contrast, placid water in long stretches.

Experienced canoeists will want to read a "Guide to White Water in Wisconsin" ($1.00), available from Wisconsin Hoofers Outing Club,

191

University of Wisconsin, Madison. The state's white-water runs are described by Andres Peekna and Richard Snellgrove, members of the club, who show the difficulty of the various sections of white water and rate according to the international scale. Factors relating to gradient, obstacles, waves, turns, and turbulence for various rivers are given.

Other Sources (Water Trails)

The American Canoe Association, 400 Eastern St., New Haven, Conn. 06500; The American Whitewater Affiliation, Harold Kiehm, 2019 W. Addison St., Chicago, Ill. 60618, and the Century Club Award Committee, 1620 Main St., Evanston, Ill. 60202, welcome queries, as do:

ALASKA Division of Lands, Dept. of Natural Resources, 344 4th Ave., Anchorage 99501.

LOUISIANA Parks and Recreation Dept., 3170 Florida St., Baton Rouge 70806.

MISSISSIPPI Park Service, State Office Bldg., Jackson 39201.

OREGON Travel Information Bureau, State Highway Dept., Salem 97310.

TEXAS Parks and Wildlife Dept., John H. Reagan Bldg., Austin 78701.

UTAH Tourist and Publicity Council, State Capitol Bldg., Salt Lake City, and State Parks and Recreation Commission, 132 South 2nd West, Salt Lake City 84101.

The above capsules virtues of various regional waters so that the canoeist bent upon adventure may select the challenge best suited to his experience, available time, and pocketbook. The omission of waterways (there are many omitted) in no ways suggests less ardor for them —the problem is simply a matter of space.

To secure information on canoeing possibilities of any state, address a letter to the Department of Tourism, Conservation, or Parks, and your inquiry will be routed to the proper agency.

MAP SOURCES

An adequate map is the first step toward adventure on any of the wide selection of waterways in the United States and Canada. The search for map sources is not so difficult for the modern canoe adventurer as it used to be. Most states and provinces, with their informational guides, their canoe outfitters, and local commercial enterprises—canoe liveries, sporting goods stores, rental agencies, gasoline companies—supply maps for the regions they serve.

Canada

An index map to the National Topographic Series (eight miles to the inch) is available from: Map Distribution Office, Department of Mines and Technical Surveys, Ottawa, Canada. From the master index map showing 17 regions, select the map (50¢ a copy) for the region that interests you. Topographical maps are available from the Map Distribution Office, 615 Booth St., Ottawa 4, Canada.

Geological maps (available for some areas) may be obtained from the Geological Survey of Canada, Ottawa, Canada.

The "Canada-United States Highway Map," showing main routes between the United States and Canada and main highways in Canada, is available from the Canadian Government Travel Bureau, Ottawa, Canada.

The Tourist Development Branch, Department of Industry and Commerce, Winnipeg, Manitoba, is another map source.

United States

Before zeroing in on your canoeing destination, get a map from any one of the major oil companies, which furnish excellent maps for routing.

The U.S. Geological Survey, Washington, D.C., is the best source of maps for comparatively small regions. Selling for less than a dollar each, these maps are available for all parts of the country, and are accurate in detail to the smallest creek. They are excellent for the canoeist, for they give a graphic picture of what he can expect on a trip. Ascertain the speed of the flow of water by the symbols indicating hills and elevations; also the mosquito havens of the lowlands, the direction of water flow (from small tributaries to larger bodies of water). One example is the map, "Superior National Forest and the Boundary Waters Canoe Area," available from the U.S. Forest Service, Milwaukee, Wisc., office. See address below.

The U.S. Forest Service, U.S. Department of Agriculture, Washington, D.C., furnishes maps for specific National Forests. The ten Forest Service regional office addresses are: (1) Federal Bldg., Missoula,

193

Mont.; (2) Federal Center, Bldg. 85, Denver, Colo.; (3) 517 Gold Ave., S.W., Albuquerque, N. Mex.; (4) Forest Service Bldg., Ogden, Utah; (5) 630 Sansome St., San Francisco, Calif.; (6) P.O. Box 3623, Portland, Ore.; (7) 6816 Market St., Upper Darby, Pa.; (8) 50 Seventh St., N.E., Atlanta, Ga.; (9) 710 N. 6th St., Milwaukee, Wisc.; (10) Fifth Street Office Bldg., P.O. Box 1631, Juneau, Alaska.

The Coast and Geodetic Survey, Department of Commerce, Washington, D.C., supplies maps for water travel: the seacoast, Ohio, and Mississippi rivers.

Interesting maps are available from the National Park Service, U.S. Department of Interior, Washington 25, D.C.

The National Park Service has established a new branch in Michigan to supervise its programs in Michigan, Indiana, Illinois, and Wisconsin. The address is 1405 S. Harrison Rd., East Lansing, Mich.

Many state highway departments furnish detailed county maps.

Maps for the Mississippi River are available from the U.S. Army Corps of Engineers, Rock Island District, Rock Island, Ill. Another source: Illinois Department of Conservation, Springfield.

The Clarkson Map Company, 724 Des Noyer St., Kaukauna, Wisc. 54130 (a private map concern) have been publishers of special-purpose maps since 1951.

Vast inland waterways—rivers, canals, intercoastal waterways, and channels, carrying 10 per cent of the freight of the United States— serve the needs of certain canoeists. The American Waterways Operators, Inc., 1250 Connecticut Ave., Washington, D.C. 20036, will answer interested commercial-waterway-artery canoeists.

The *Guidebook to Campgrounds,* issued annually by Rand McNally ($3.95), is available from your local bookstore or from one of the offices of the publisher: 405 Park Ave., New York, N.Y. 10022; P.O. Box 7600, Chicago, Ill. 60680; and 423 Market St., San Francisco, Calif. 94105. Approximately 12,000 campgrounds with 450,000 campsites are star-rated, and each is numbered, with the number of the camp appearing on the adjacent state or province map (from which canoeists can see their proximity to water). The numbered listing indicates name and address of the campground, access highways and roads, size (in acres), number of tent sites, daily fee, season dates, time limit, admission of pets. Facilities indicated are: trailer space, tables, firewood, kitchen shelter, shelters, change house, flush toilets, showers, and whether or not the following are on the campground or within one mile: ice, laundry, cafe or snack bar, store. Activities checked are: hiking, swimming, fishing, playground, and rental and/or launching of boats. State, provincial, and territorial parks, forests and recreation areas, national parks and forest, as well as campgrounds administered by the Wildlife Service, Bureau of Reclamation, Army Corps of Engineers, Bureau of Land Management, Bureau of Indian Affairs and TVA, as well as many private, city, and county grounds are included. Because approximately 1,000 campgrounds are added each year, Rand McNally urge campers to write well in advance to confirm facilities and to make reservations. They publish similar guides: *Travel Trailer Guide, National Park Guide* (full-color illustrated with pictures worth framing), *Vacation Guide,* and road atlases.

WARNING

Stream conditions can change from year to year, season to season, even from day to day: a recommendation from one party to another could be invalid immediately after being given.

Privately owned streams should be used only with the permission of the riparian owners, and all essentials—campsites, water, and wood supplies—must be worked out with owners prior to any trips through private lands.

On average canoe trips, it is never necessary to carry firearms. Anyone familiar with literature on outdoor life knows of many incidents— harrowing and sometimes fatal—of an animal's being wounded from gunfire, yet not too weak to eliminate its tormentor or to send him screaming up a tree, to remain there for days!

FINALE

New canoe trails are discovered largely by canoeists who report stream conditions, put-in and take-out points, number of miles, paddling times, depth, current, bottom, banks, water conditions, etc., to representatives of state agencies. Be the first in your state to discover an interesting water route: perhaps it will be named for you.

21

Bon Voyage!

Man's urge to respond to the eternal lure of the mystery of moving water at times when he wishes a contrast to high speed and to air travel, and desires to strip life to its essentials and to leave behind the pampering comforts of civilization, has led to a rediscovery of the sport of canoeing. The recreational, body-building, social, and intellectual values of canoeing and camping have not lessened in this space age; they are more important than ever.

It is still possible in the latter part of the twentieth century, in out-of-the-way canoe country, to dip from a lake and drink the cool, sweet, pure water, hear the haunting cry of the loon, observe the whiskey-jack's delinquencies, surprise moose in weedy bays, watch beavers at work and otters sliding down steep banks, and to commune with great lonely rivers and silent granite hills—and gain a personal contentment, for happiness is losing yourself in something bigger than yourself.

What other experience commands such complete involvement with life-sustaining activities as does a canoe-camping experience? Each member of the group understands what has to be done for safety, survival, and satisfaction. Creative cooperation becomes a matter of the spirit—above the world, above any kind of physical juxtaposition— far above any earthly plane. As you sprawl around the campfire at night and sing songs that have grown out of pioneer life, you identify with those who have traveled the way before and who have found meaning in their lives and in the direction of life.

In the deep recesses of one's being, every canoeist wishes he could grasp the moment and never let it slip, wishes that everyone, everywhere, could know this experience of nature as is his privilege. He hopes that it will remain for his children, and for their children, ravaged by neither time nor man.

Yet, at home, one has but to pick up a newspaper or listen to a broadcast to learn that man has polluted, unthinkingly, the Great Lakes and all the major rivers of America and Europe, and to realize that the balance of nature (ecology) is seriously threatened in such remote areas as the far Antarctic, the Aldabra Atoll in the Indian Ocean, and the jungles of South America. Many man-ravaged natural environments peril the very existence of all species of plant and animal life.

The outlook for improved canoeing (also fishing and camping), however, is heartening. Under the Land and Water Conservation Act, the federal government offers matching money grants to state and local agencies that meet fund requirements and other stipulations to qualify for federal assistance. The Act, aimed primarily at water- and air-pollution control improvement, also carries, as fringe benefits, the upgrading and expansion of outdoor recreation. For example, both New York and Pennsylvania have budgeted $200 million to be spent over several years for recreational facilities.

Aware of his stake in the responsibility for, and guardianship of, his natural heritage, the dedicated canoeist writes to elected officials, to newspapers, magazines, and his State Conservation Commission, telling them his observations and opinions: he reports littered waters and shorelines to local authorities as well as to national agencies (personal, hand-written letters are better than mimeographed material). He remembers that Scouts often engage in clean-up campaigns, and they can be called upon to participate in clean-stream programs.

A dedicated canoeist becomes an active member of a conservation organization, such as a local and/or national group: for example, in the United States, the Audubon Society, the Sierra and Alpine clubs, the Wilderness or Wild Life Association, the Izaak Walton League, and others listed.

All purposeful activities are first instigated on the planes of spiritual creativity, awaiting those who are receptive and willing to receive their impulses—and who make themselves capable of receiving them. Confident that you are making your contribution to conservation, somewhere along the water trails you will pass a point, neither in time nor space, when you will be linked with the eternal, where only you and a Greater Force abide. You will feel that time has stopped, and the rhythms of nature have taken over—and you discover perfect peace. You will feel like the cloud islands in the sky, separated from the world and existing only in the present moment, and you will savor it, and it will sustain you when you are away from your beloved Shangri-La.

APPENDIX

A Personal Conditioning Program for Canoeists

by Jim Descourouez
Assistant Professor of Physical Education for Men
University of Illinois at Chicago Circle
(Head Trainer, Corrective Therapist)

Unless the muscles involved in executing the paddling strokes have been conditioned (built up) before the paddling season, parts of a canoeist's body may be stiff and sore after a canoeing excursion.

Aware that all team sports include an annual training period, the serious canoeist, experienced as well as beginner, having a general knowledge of the muscles used in the various paddling strokes, understands the value of a personal conditioning program (on an out-of-season basis) that emphasizes building up areas of the muscles involved.

Note: All strokes are herein analyzed (kinesiologically) as right-sided movement (starboard stroke). Since all strokes are executed on either side of the canoe, build up for left-sided (portside stroke) movement simply by interchanging the instruction "left" for "right," and vice versa.

THE BOW STROKE

Top (left) Arm
Hand and Wrist—Hold firmly on paddle grip.
Elbow   —Start flexed at shoulder height.
                 Action—Punch-type extension.
                 Muscles—Triceps.

Shoulder —Start abducted and flexed.
Action—Depressed across in front of body.
Muscles—Pectoralis major and minor, Latissimus dorsi, and Teres major.

Bottom (right) arm
Hand and Wrist—Hold firmly on throat of paddle.
Elbow —Start extended.
Action—Pull into slight flexion.
Muscles—Biceps, Brachialis, Brachioradialis
Shoulder —Start flexed and slightly abducted.
Action—Abduction moving into hyperextension.
Muscles—Latissimus dorsi, Teres major, and Posterior deltoid.

Remember—All the major back muscles play a large role in executing the bow stroke. These muscles are Latissimus dorsi, Teres major, Infraspinatus, Posterior deltoid, Rhomboid group, and Trapezius.

J STROKE

Top Arm—Same as Bow Stroke.
Bottom (right) Arm
Hand and Wrist—Hold firmly on throat of paddle.
Action—Roll wrist into flexion, and forearm pulls into slight pronation.
Muscles—Flexor carpi ulnaris, Flexor carpi radialis, Palmaris longus.
Pronation—Pronator quadratus and Pronator teres.
Elbow —Start extended.
Action—Pull into flexion.
Muscles—Biceps, Brachialis, and Brachioradialis.
Shoulder —Start flexed and slightly abducted.
Action—Depression and pull past the body, also inward rotation.
Muscles—Deltoid, Latissimus dorsi, Teres major, Subscapularis, and Trapezius.

200

FEATHERING

Top Arm
Hand and Wrist—Hold firmly on grip.
Elbow —Start extended across in front of body.
Action—Move into flexion and raise upward.
Muscles—Biceps, Brachialis, Brachioradialis.
Shoulder —Start depressed in front of the body.
Action—Move upward and outward in a horizontal abducting movement.
Muscles—Posterior deltoid, Infraspinatus, and Teres minor.

Bottom Arm
Hand and Wrist—Hold firmly on the throat of paddle.
Action—Flexion and some pronation.
Muscles—Flexor carpi ulnaris, Flexor carpi radialis, Palmaris longus, Pronator quadratus, and Pronator teres.
Elbow —Slight flexion.
Action—Pull into extension.
Muscles—Triceps.
Shoulder —Depressed behind the body.
Action—Upward and forward in a form of horizontal abduction.
Muscles—Anterior deltoid, Subscapularis, Pectoralis major, and Coracobrachialis.

CANADIAN GUIDE STROKE

Same as the J Stroke, with the following exceptions:
Top Arm
Shoulder —Depressed across in front of the body, but out away from the body.
Action—Start flexed and abducted.
Muscles—More Anterior deltoid and less Pectoralis.

Bottom Arm
Hand and Wrist—Hand held firm.
Action—Little or no flexion and pronation.
Elbow —Pulls into slight flexion.

Shoulder —Moves into slight abduction, keeping the arm out and away from the body.
Muscles—Middle deltoid and Supraspinatus.

QUARTER SWEEP (BOWMAN)

Top Arm
Hand and Wrist—Hold firmly on grip.
Elbow —Deeply flexed.
Action—Push into extension.
Muscles—Triceps.
Shoulder —Abduction and horizontal extension.
Action—Move into horizontal flexion and slight depression.
Muscles—Deltoid, Pectoralis, and Subscapularis.
Bottom Arm
Hand and Wrist—Hold firmly on throat of paddle.
Elbow —Hold in flexion.
Shoulder —Hold in slight abduction with some hyperextension.
Action—Little or none.

REVERSE SWEEP

This is exactly the opposite of the quarter sweep in that the top arm pulls into flexion, and the shoulder extends horizontally.

DRAW STROKE

Top Arm
Hand and Wrist—Hold firmly on grip.
Elbow —Extended across in front of chest.
Action—Pull into slight flexion.
Muscles—Biceps.
Shoulder —Horizontally flexed in front of the chest.
Action—Some depression and slight horizontal extension.
Muscles—Deltoid, Pectoralis, Teres major, and Infraspinatus.

Bottom Arm

Hand and Wrist—Extended.

                    Action—Pull into flexion and hold firm.

                    Muscles—Flexor carpi ulnaris, Flexor carpi radialis, and Palmaris longus.

Elbow   —Extend fully.

                    Action—Pulling into flexion.

                    Muscles—Biceps.

Shoulder   —Abduction.

                    Action—Abducting and hyperextending.

                    Muscles—Latissimus dorsi, Teres major, and Pectoralis major.

JAM (STOPPING AND HOLDING) STROKE

This is a holding position with most of the joints and muscles held in a static contraction.

Hands and Wrists—Hold firmly on grip.

Elbows   —Slightly flexed.

Shoulders   —Set firmly: however, back muscles play an important part in holding.

BACKWATER STROKE

Top Arm

Hand and Wrist—Hold firmly on grip.

Elbow   —Almost fully extended.

                    Action—Pull into flexion.

                    Muscles—Biceps.

Shoulder   —Horizontal adduction across in front of the chest.

                    Action—Move into horizontal hyperextension and slight depression.

                    Muscles—Deltoid and Latissimus dorsi.

Bottom Arm

Hand and Wrist—Hold firmly on grip.

Elbow   —Deep flexion.

                    Action—Push into extension.

                    Muscles—Triceps.

Shoulder —Deep hyperextension.
Action—Push into flexion.
Muscles—Pectoralis major, Deltoid, and Teres major.

SCULLING STROKE

Top Arm

Hand and Wrist—Hold firmly on grip.
Action—Ulnar and radial flexion.
Muscles—Extensor carpi ulnaris, Flexor carpi ulnaris, Extensor carpi radialis longus, Extensor carpi radialis brevis.
Elbow —Hold in slight extension.
Shoulder —Hold in horizontal adduction across the chest.

Bottom Arm

Hand and Wrist—Hold firmly on grip.
Action—Flexion and extension.
Muscles—Flexor carpi ulnaris, Flexor carpi radialis, Palmaris longus, Extensor carpi radialis longus, Extensor carpi radialis brevis, and Extensor carpi ulnaris.
Elbow —Hold in slight flexion.
Shoulder —Starts in abduction.
Action—Move from flexion to hyperextension as the arm moves from abduction to adduction.
Muscles—Deltoid, Pectoralis major, Supraspinatus, Latissimus dorsi, and Teres major.

Throughout all canoeing strokes, the shoulder girdle takes an active part. The shoulder routine will develop other shoulder muscles as well as those mentioned.

CONDITIONING-FOR-CANOEING EXERCISES

This conditioning program is designed to develop and to strengthen the various parts of the body used in canoeing. Each set of exercises has been developed into three successive stages: Mild, Moderate, and Heavy.

The Mild Form, needing little or no equipment, develops range of motion and some muscle tone.

The Moderate Form increases the range of motion and develops some strength. The repetitions are increased, and some type of resistance is used.

The Heavy Form develops the full range of motion and maximum strength. This form uses greatest resistance and the largest number of repetitions.

The exercises are broken down in relation to the various parts of the body.

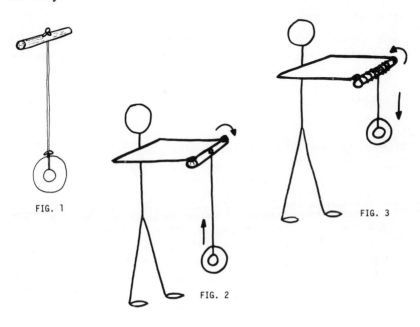

FIG. 1

FIG. 2

FIG. 3

Hand, Wrist, and Forearm

Mild Exercise. Squeeze a handful of modeling clay, starting with 5 to 10 repetitions, and increasing the number as the grip feels stronger.

Moderate Exercise. Squeeze a rubber ball (a tennis ball is adequate) starting with 5 to 10 repetitions, increasing the number as strength develops.

Heavy Exercise. Use a wrist roller, a round piece of wood about 15 inches long and at least 4 to 6 inches in circumference (a broken paddle shaft will do), to simulate the throat of a paddle. Drill a hole through the roller, along the line of the diameter, at the center of the roller. Push a 4-foot piece of clothesline through the hole. Tie a knot at one end to keep the line or rope from falling out (SEE FIGURE 1).

Hold the roller with both hands (backs of hands up), arms extended. Turn the roller to wind the rope around the roller, turning away from body (SEE FIGURE 2). Then reverse the action to unwind the rope (SEE FIGURE 3). Repeat this winding and unwinding exercise 10 or 20 times to start. As strength develops, tie a 5-lb. weight to the end of the rope, and, as strength warrants, further increase the number of repetitions and the weight.

Elbow and Shoulder

Mild Exercise. Do push-ups while kneeling. SEE FIGURE 4. For more strength, stop and hold the exercise at various positions both pushing up and lowering the body. SEE FIGURE 5.

Moderate Exercise. Do a regular push-up 10 to 30 times. As in the Mild Exercises, more strength will develop by holding the body

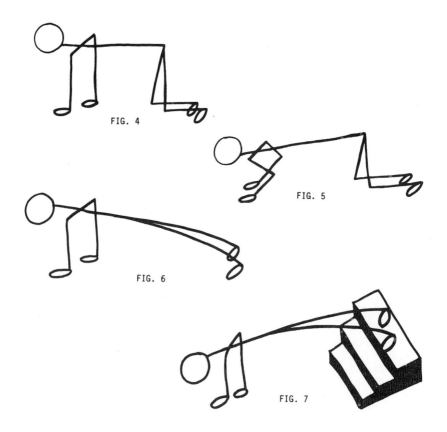

FIG. 4

FIG. 5

FIG. 6

FIG. 7

at various levels in a static contraction. These variations will improve your ability to brake and to hold the canoe. SEE FIGURE 6.

Heavy Exercise. Do several push-ups with your feet up on a low stool or the first or second step of a staircase. SEE FIGURE 7.

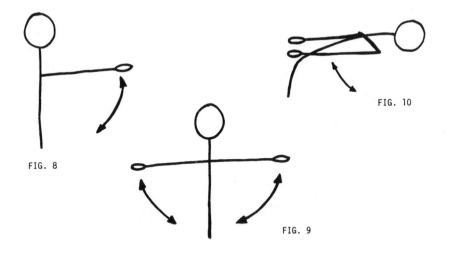

FIG. 10

FIG. 8

FIG. 9

Total Shoulder–Basic Shoulder Routine

Mild Exercise. The following exercises with no weight and 5 to 10 repetitions.

Moderate Exercise. The following exercises with 5 to 7 pounds of weight and 30 repetitions (three sets of 10 each).

Heavy Exercise. The following exercise with 10 pounds of weight and up to 50 repetitions.

EXERCISE NO. 1. Start in a standing position with arms at sides (military stance). Swing both arms forward to a position parallel with the floor, but not above shoulder level. Slowly return the arms to the starting position. SEE FIGURE 8.

EXERCISE NO. 2. Assume a military stance. Raise your arms slowly to your sides, palms down, to a position parallel to the floor, and slowly return to the starting position. SEE FIGURE 9.

EXERCISE NO. 3. Bend forward at the waist and place your hands on the knees. Then let your arms hang down relaxed under your shoulders. Pull both arms up alongside your body. It is very important that your arms stay along the side and do not fly out away from your body. Slowly return to the starting position. SEE FIGURE 10.

EXERCISE NO. 4. Lying on your back on the floor, assume a starting position with your arms outstretched, forming a "T" with the trunk of your body. Raise both arms upward at right angles to the floor, parallel to each other, keeping the elbows extended. SEE FIGURE 11. Lower arms to the starting position.

EXERCISE NO. 5. Assume a starting position face down on a table or bench. This also can be done by resting your chest on the seat of a chair and kneeling on the floor. At right angles to the spine, at shoulder level, hang your arms down toward the floor, extended at the elbow. Raise arms up sideward as far as possible and slowly return. SEE FIGURE 12.

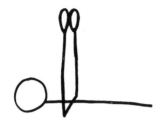

FIG. 11

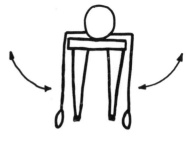

FIG. 12

FIG. 13

FIG. 14

208

Shoulder Girdle and Upper Back

Mild Exercise. Standing in a military position without weights, pull up and roll shoulders forward, and let them down to a starting position. Next, pull up and roll shoulders backward down to starting position. SEE FIGURE 13.

Moderate Exercise. Same as Mild Exercise with 5 to 10 pounds in each hand.

Heavy Exercise. Same as Mild Exercise, with up to 25 pounds in each hand, and then use a barbell. The basic exercise remains the same.

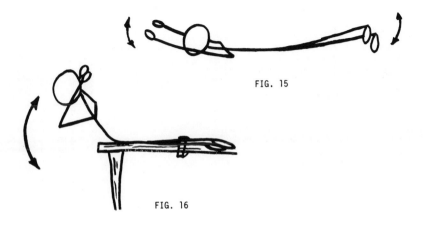

FIG. 15

FIG. 16

Total Back

Mild Exercise. On hands and knees, assume a sway-backed position. Bow your back up as high as possible, like an angry cat. SEE FIGURE 14.

Moderate Exercise. Lying on the floor face down, raise up both arms and legs as high as possible. For further development, hold this position and rock on your stomach. For a variation, raise opposite arm and leg. SEE FIGURE 15.

Heavy Exercise. Assume a position face down with waist, hips, and legs on a table or bench and arms in a push-up position on the floor. Have someone sit on the table to hold your legs, or use a seat belt or strap. Placing your hands behind the head, arch your back, pulling head and shoulders up as high as possible. Slowly return and repeat 10 to 15 times. SEE FIGURE 16.

209

Index

INDEX